THE LIFE OF
ST. SAMUEL
OF KALAMUN

SAINT **SHENOUDA**PRESS

THE LIFE OF
ST. SAMUEL
OF KALAMUN

ISAAC THE PRESBYTER

EDITED & TRANSLATED BY

ANTHONY ALCOCK

ST SHENOUDA PRESS
SYDNEY, AUSTRALIA
2020

THE LIFE OF ST SAMUEL OF KALAMUN

Isaac the Presbyter

Edited & Translated by Anthony Alcock

ST SHENOUDA PRESS
8419 Putty Rd,
Putty, NSW, 2330
Sydney, Australia

www.stshenoudapress.com

ISBN 13: 978-0-6488658-5-8

Cover Design: Dionysia Tanios
@dionysiandesigns

Contents

PREFACE

I wish to thank the following libraries for giving me permission to publish material in their collections: the Pierpont Morgan Library, New York, the Bodleian Library, Oxford, and the National Libraries in Naples, Paris and Vienna. I wish to thank colleagues and friends who have offered assistance and advice. Finally, I wish to thank St Shenouda Press for agreeing to publish the work. I accept sole responsibility for the errors.

Anthony Alcock

INTRODUCTION

There are four versions of the Life of Samuel:

a)   the Pierpont Morgan Ms. 578 ff. 1-68, which is complete

b)   a fragmentary Sahidic version

c)   a fragmentary Bohairic version[1]

d)   a complete Ethiopic version, which has been edited and translated by F. Pereira *Vida do Abba Samuel.*

In this book I shall deal with only the first two versions, and for the sake of convenience they are called Codex A and B, respectively.

Codex A has been described by Hyvernat in his as follows: "Synaxary. Isaac of Kalamon. IX cent. 68 leaves; 2 columns of 28-33 lines. 340x355cm." It is not, however, the only text in Ms. 578.[2]

---

1   One has been published by Crum in *Catalogue of Coptic mss. in the British Museum* (London, 1905) no.917; the other is unpublished, but has been described by Burmester in *Koptische Hss.1: die Hss.der Staatsbibliothek Hamburg* (Wiesbaden,1975) p.306. I have looked at a slide of the latter, but the ink is very faint.

2   In the same ms. are the *Sermon on the Patriarch Joseph* by Ephrem and the *Paralipomena of Jeremiah* (edited and translated by K.H.Kuhn in *Le Muséon* vol.83.

An attempt to date it more precisely than Hyvernat has been made by Th. Petersen[3], who suggests that the ornamentation resembles that of Ms.612, datable by its colophon to 892-3[4], so closely that the two Mss. must have been written by the same scribe.

I think there is room for doubt, though on palaeographical grounds a 9th cent. date is not impossible. Since I have been able to consult only a xerographic copy of the photographic edition made by Hyvernat *Bibliothecae Pierpont Morgan codices coptici photographice expressi* (Rome, 1922) v.31, I hesitate to attempt a full description of the ornamentation, but the top of the first page is clearly decorated with plait and scroll work and vine tendrils, the ends of which are being chewed by an animal, probably a hare.

Codex B consists of nine fragments[5], and they have the following inventory numbers:

fr. 1 : Naples I.B.8 400

fr. 2 : Naples I.B.8 400

fr. 3 : Clar. Press b.5 no, 60

fr. 4 : Naples I.B.8 400

fr. 5 : Naples I.B.8 400

fr. 6 : Naples I.B.8 400

fr. 7 : Paris 129[13] fol.30

---

3   cf. *Studies presented to Bella da Costa Greene* p.317.

4   cf. A.van Lantschoot *Receuil des colophons coptes* p.28ff.

5   Nine fragments of the *Life* were published by Amélineau in *Monuments* p.770-789; his fr. no.V is not in fact part of the *Life*, but part of a homily on Samuel, fragments of which have been published by Simon in *Miscellanea Biblica*. (I intend to re-edit all of these fragments at a later date.) He obviously did not have a chance to consult the Vienna fr., first published by Wessely in *Griechische und Koptische Texte* iv Leipzig, 1914) no.194.

fr. 8 : Vienna K 342

fr. 9 : this was originally in Cairo, subsequently transferred to Louvain and destroyed there during World War Two.[6] The only extant copy is that made by Amélineau and is no. IX in Monuments.

It is clear from a comparison of the two versions that Codex B is much fuller in places than A and to judge from the pagination is about 30 pages longer.

Codex A, like most of the Morgan Mss., is written in Sahidic, but exhibits non-Sahidic characteristics; they may be due to the native dialect of the scribe, Fayyumic[7].

Samuel was born into a wealthy family c.597 in the N.E. Delta and died c.695 in his monastery at Kalamun, traditionally located in the N.E. of the Wadi Mouellah (but cf. n.248 of the text). I shall try only to summarise the contents of this *Life*, and for an account of the prevailing political and ecclesiastical conditions I would recommend the reader to consult c.9 of Frend's *Rise of the Monophysite movement*.

The title of the *Life* reveals that it was written in response to popular demand by the presbyter Isaac of Kalamun. In a lengthy introduction Isaac declares that he has been guided by the oral tradition of four generations (indicating perhaps that the first recension may be dated to the first half of the 9th century?). He recounts Samuel's early insistence on becoming a monk and the eventual acceptance of this desire by his parents, Silas and Kosmiane, of whom the latter dies when Samuel is eighteen.

---

6 This text is described by Lefort in *Les manuscrits coptes de l'JJniversite de Louvain* (Louvain, 1940) no.40. I was informed by letter that the ms. was no longer extant and had probably perished in World War Two.

7 For other surveys of this mixed dialect cf. Kuhn *Panegyric* xiv-xv and Quecke *Stundengebet* 359ff. The latter has a particularly informative section on the use of the supralinear stroke, which is relatively common in this text and is near the fully developed pointing system in Bohairic.

Silas, evidently not certain of his son's wish for the monastic life, is visited by an angel, who assures him of Samuel's intention; in gratitude Silas builds a church and ordains his son (already a sub-deacon at twelve) a deacon of it. Samuel is twenty-two when his father dies. Samuel subsequently sets out for that centre of monasticism, Scetis, and, with the assistance of an angel, is introduced to an aged ascete, Agathou, who occupies a cave between the monasteries of Macrius and John.

After three years' training with his master, Samuel is once again bereaved, but receives strength from the spirit of the deceased Agathou, like Elisha from Elijah, with the result that his fame spreads and he becomes a monk of consequence in Scetis. Cyrus the Bishop of Phasis arrives to occupy the See of Alexandria and take over the civil administration of Egypt: his principal duty is to reconcile the largely Monophysite Copts to Constantinople by means of a new Christological doctrine emphasising the 'one energy' of Christ. The Copts refuse to accept it (in fact, it is referred to constantly in the *Life* as the 'Tome of Leo', an indication perhaps that they did not understand the full import of this subtle new doctrine. Cyrus' agent arrives at Scetis with this document; as spokesman for the community, Samuel asks if he may consult it; once in possession of it, however, he tears it to shreds and is severely flogged by the agent as a result. Expelled from Scetis, Samuel journeys south with four disciples and is received into the monastery of Neklone.

After three and a half years there, he hears that Cyrus is coming in person to the Fayyum and orders the monks to evacuate the place. When Cyrus learns what Samuel has done, he has him arrested for a traitor and, after a 'martyrological' exchange, beaten to within an inch of his life. Samuel goes from Neklone to Takinash, where he spends six months before being summoned, like Abraham, by the voice of God to go forth into the wilderness. He arrives at a deserted church in Kalamun. On their way home from pillage, marauding Libyan nomads seize him in the church and set him on a camel with the intention of taking him with them. However, the camel, inspired by God, obstinately refuses to move. The Berbers abandon the saint.

But on their next visit the Berbers are more successful and carry him off to Siwa, where they sell him into slavery and he meets a former colleague, John the Hegumen of Scetis, also enslaved. During a three year captivity, attempts are made to compel the saint to accept paganism and abandon his chastity, but he withstands them. As a reward, he is given the power by God to work miracles; and the Berbers, sensing a threat from this 'man of heaven', wisely agree to release him. Back at Kalamun with gifts of fine camels from his captors, Samuel receives his original four disciples and many others from neighbouring monasteries. The community thrives. The monastery accepts donations and is particularly fortunate in receiving large ones from the ill-tempered and miserly Bishop Gregory of Koeis and Mena the Eparch of Pelhip, a relative (?) of Samuel. No small contribution is made to the monastery's prosperity by Apollo, Samuel's 'Jesse', who is responsible for the commercial relations of the community. Samuel spends a total of fifty seven years at Kalamun.

The document described above is a straightforward hagiography, but embedded in it is a martyrology: twice the holy man is saluted as the 'one who became a martyr without his head being removed and 'the one who became a martyr many times without shedding his blood' though this latter description is not strictly accurate, for Samuel appears to have shed a large quantity of it at the hands of Cyrus and his agent. The interviews between Samuel and both of these are remarkably similar to those between the martyr and pagan governor in earlier martyrological texts, but, unlike those sometimes wondrous documents, this text tends to be more sober in its description of the pain felt by the saint after his punishment. Perhaps this concession to reality is dictated by the unpleasant fact that, whereas pagan governors were idolaters who could not be expected to know any better than to inflict punishment on a man of God, the latter-day persecutors were fellow Christians, who knew precisely what they were doing.

Finally, I should like to say something about the presentation of the texts. Both codices were originally written in columns, two to a page. For reasons of convenience and economy, I have presented both in continuous form and employed the device of dividing the text into numbered chapters, which correspond to nothing more than my own notion of how the text might be analysed. I have tried to retain the punctuation of the original, but have simplified all 'paragraph' endings to:- . Wherever possible the supralinear stroke has been reproduced, even though in many cases this is no more than a dot. I present the original page numbers between two strokes | |, including the quire numbers as appropriate. I have not given the folio numbers.

THE LIFE OF SAMUEL OF KALAMUN

THIS IS THE LIFE AND CONDUCT OF OUR HOLY AND REVERED father, the *anchorite* and *archimandrite* Apa Samuel, the father of the holy *Community* of the *Virgin*[8] of the mountain of Kalamun in the province of the Fayyum, *narrated* by the God loving *presbyter* and *ascete* of this same mountain of Kalamun, Apa Isaac, because some God-loving men and holy elders *urged* him to do this. He began with great *zeal* and recited some few of the sufferings which he underwent and he *started* from his birth to his death. He delivered it (i.e. the 10 recitation) because it was the day of his holy commemoration, that is, the 8th of Khoiak[9] in the peace of God. Amen.

1.   FOR TRULY I HAVE BEGUN TO STIR THE ORGAN OF MY weak tongue[10] in a *spiritual* movement. My *reason* moves me, lifting up my *mind* in solicitude and summoning me in great

---

8   1. i.e. the Virgin Mary. Samuel had a special relationship with the B.V.Mary: it was on the day of the Assumption that he first left his disciples to go into the desert and eventually find Kalamun (p. 86); after his captivity and return to Kalamun the B.V.Mary appeared to the saint in the church, promising that she 'Would remain with him forever' (p.101); Samuel insisted that the first church to be built at Kalamun since his occupation of it be dedicated to the B.V.Mary (pl06).

9   Dec. 4th.

10   For a parallel usage cf. Budge *Coptic Martyrdoms* p. 138.

joy *be-fitting* the memory of the *ascetic life* of the *one who bears* God in truth, the *defender* of the piety of *monkhood*, the holy *champion*, Apa Samuel, the father of the holy *Community* of the *Virgin* of Kalamun in the province of the Fayyum.

I look to the loftiness of his spiritual conduct[11] and his *angelic life* and I pay attention in profound obedience to many testimonies, which *instruct* us in a great *instruction* teaching me of all the works of *blessedness* of his *pious life* that is, the testimony of our holy fathers who have spent the entire period of their life with their *hope* in the truth. *Moreover*, they also, our holy fathers, heard from their fathers who were before them, and they heard from their fathers, who *were the disciples* of that great one, Apa Samuel. *Furthermore*, those who have seen with their eyes and heard with their ears, their hands have touched him[12], confirmed in their belief about everything that happened to the *righteous one* and *having instructed* their children with confirmed testimony, even unto their children and grandchildren, that is, our revered *spiritual* fathers, at whose feet we sat and who told us everything, *according* as it is written in the Book of Psalms[13], "The things which we have heard, we have known them, and the things which our fathers told us, they have not concealed them from their sons for another generation, speaking of the blessings and miracles of the Lord and the wonders He performed."

Therefore, I, the *meanest* sinner, I *believe*, and more than *believe*, *attending to* what my fathers have testified concerning our *righteous* father Apa Samuel, whose feast we commemorate today. I hear from them about the fame of his great *feats of asceticism* and wonderful and *successful virtues* of that great and *perfect* man

---

11   cf. Heb.13, 7.

12   cf. John 1, 1. I am not certain of the translation, but I understand the object of 'touched' to be Samuel.

13   cf.Ps.78, 3.

of God, Apa Samuel, this one, whose *life* and whose *conduct* are equal to those of the great Antony[14].

Therefore, since I hear of the fame of his *conduct, virtues* and his wonderful *ascetic practices*, in which he *struggled* with great fortitude, *especially* also his deeds which shine like the stars of heaven, I *am at a loss* in my heart and often hesitate as I approach the *narration* of his *life*. Because of the poverty of my *mind* and the feebleness of my tongue, I reproach myself, saying, "What is the use of an *idiot* like me approaching this great *sea* which is revealed and full of every *good thing*, that is, the *life* of this great shining *beacon*, our father Apa Samuel, the *narration* of whose *life requires* a *wise* man, whose *mind* shines clearly and who has *faith* in the saints?" *But* after all this, because of the *joy* of this great feast today and the commemoration of our *champion* Apa Samuel, I will take to myself the encouragement of his holy prayers and proceed to the *debt* which I owe and *begin* his *life*, from *beginning* to end. Come then, give me the *assembled strength* of your holy prayers so that we may *inform* you *to* the extent of our poverty (i.e. of wit) *according* to what the word will teach us.

2.   AS TO THE HOMELAND OF THE HOLY APA SAMUEL, HE was a man of the north *country*, belonging to the *neighbourhood* of the *city* of Pelhip from the village of Tkello[15]. *But rather* his *true homeland* was the heavenly Jerusalem[16]. The holy Apa Samuel was the son of a God-loving *presbyter*, whose name was Silas. The name of his *blessed* mother was Kosmiane. These were wealthy people *according* to this *world, but* poor in spirit, like the *patriarch* Abraham[17], and they spent most of their wealth for the

---

14   Antony, the traditional founder of monasticism (251-356). On two occasions Samuel is confronted by the devil, who tells the saint angrily that he is 'following the example of Antony' (p. 87) and asks him whose example he is following (p.112).

15   The city of Pelhip was in the N.E.Delta cf. Amelineau *Geog. de l'Egypte* 314.

16   cf. Heb.12, 22.

17   Might this be a mixed allusion to Matt.3, 2 (poor=humble) and Gen.18, where Abraham's generosity is described?

benefit of the poor to the glory of God and His *Christ*, because they were hospitable to strangers and the poor, taking care of everyone who *needed* it, like the *righteous* Job[18].

Most of their rooms[19] were places of sojourn for strangers, the sick, the weak, the blind, the infirm aged and orphans, and they *attended* them with great *care* for the *love* of *Christ*, keeping all the *commandments* of the *Gospel*, being perfect in every act of mercy. The sweet odour of their wealth was diffused on the lips of everyone, and they were blessed by the poor of their district. *In a word*, their acts of *charity* and mercy in prisons and *hospitals* were so regular *that* the sweet odour of their *charity* reached everywhere. *But* the holy Silas and his *blessed* wife were greatly advanced in their old age and were near the end of their days, and they had no other children *but* the holy Samuel. *Now* he was a *subdeacon* at the age of twelve. His parents had brought him up to love God with *calm* and wisdom, and God had *granted* him *wisdom* like that of Solomon, the son of David.

He would *fast* every day until evening bound to the house of God[20] day and night. He would not drink wine or eat meat or anything from which blood came. His parents used to approach him with words of *flattery* and supplication with the intention of *persuading* him to take a wife in *holy matrimony according* to this *world*[21]. He refused to *obey* them, *but* he would say, "I wish to go and become a *monk*." And if they continued to *bother* him about this, he would weep and say to them, "If you do not stop *distressing* me, then I shall go away and become a monk[22]. I shall

---

18 cf. Job 29,16.

19 Were these apartment houses?

20 The same phrase occurs in Kuhn Panegyric p.4,32.

21 This phrase will serve to distinguish earthly marriage from the higher marriage to the service of God.

22 I have not translated the Gk. word : it could mean 'forthwith', but I think the meaning suggested by Lee in Muséon 83,137 'perhaps' is more appropriate. In support of his suggestion he cites an interesting parallel in Romanian.

leave you, and you will never see me again." When they saw him weeping, they were very *distressed*, and his mother would approach him, weeping, and embrace him about the neck and kiss him on the mouth, head and breast, saying, "Stop crying and grieving myself and your aged father. *But* if it is your wish to become a *monk*, we rejoice with you and are very happy if indeed God will make us worthy of a *seed* in Sion and a relative in heavenly Jerusalem." Then after a few days his *blessed* mother Kosmiane went to rest in *peace*. *Now* she left the holy Apa Samuel when he was eighteen years old.

3. THE HOLY SILAS, HIS FATHER, WAS VERY SOLICITOUS about the holy Samuel, his son, for he did not know whether he would become a *monk* or not. Therefore he saw a *vision* in a revelation at the third hour of the day[23]. Behold an *angel* appeared to him in joy and said to him, "Hail, Silas the *presbyter*, have courage and do not be afraid. The Lord is with you, and your son Samuel will become a *monk* and a great one in the sight of God. The memory of his *monkhood* will remain for *generations* to come. The Lord God will bless him and he will have holy children and there will be holy *anchorites* among them, faithful in the sight of God, and there will be *good* shepherds and *hegumens* among them. You, Silas the *presbyter*, take care of your house, for the days of your life have drawn near to the time when you will go to the Lord."

When he had said these things to him, the *angel* of the Lord disappeared from him, and when Silas the *presbyter* had *recovered* from the *vision*, he was deeply joyous and his heart was content with what he had heard from the *angel* of the Lord. He thought to himself, "Behold, I know what I shall do. I shall go forth, God willing, and build a great *church*. Everything that I have I shall donate to it." And he began building the church. He *adorned* it with every beautiful thing.

---

23 9 a.m.

Within two complete years he finished it in all (its) beauty and gave all he had to it. He ordained the holy Apa Samuel *deacon* and placed him in the *church*, still a *virgin*. Then after this the holy Silas also went to rest at a ripe old age, and he left Samuel alone, who was *now* twenty-two years old[24]. It happened after the death of his father that the holy Apa Samuel *then* retired into great seclusion for some days.

4.   AFTERWARDS HE PRAYED AND PREPARED HIMSELF TO GO to the mountain of Scetis[25] in great joy, with the *angel* of the Lord as his companion. The angel of the Lord appeared to him in the guise of a hoary old man and said to him, "Young man, whence have you come and where are you going?" The holy Apa Samuel said to him, "I have come from my village and my province and I wish to go to Scetis to become a *monk*." The *angel* replied, "Look here, I shall accompany you to that place. I have *important* business there, and this is why I shall come (with you)." The holy Apa Samuel rejoiced greatly and worshipped the *angel* and received his blessing, saying, "God has looked upon my exile[26] and has sent you to me so that you may be a father to me until I come to Scetis."

And so they prayed together and set out on their journey, and the *angel* of the Lord began to instruct him gently[27], teaching him about the works of *monkhood*. *Then*, after six days they *reached*, the vicinity of Apa Macarius the Great, the *spirit-bearer*,

---

24 Some confusion has arisen in Isaac's mind about when Samuel became a monk, for in his summary he records that Samuel did so when he was eighteen (p.115). In fact he had merely resolved to do so at that age.

25 Scetis was a centre of Egyptian monasticism; its modern name is Wadi Natrun, about 80km NW of Cairo.

26 Exile or 'the condition of being a stranger' was considered the equivalent of martyrdom by the Copts cf. Reymond and Barns Four Coptic Martyrdoms pp.5, 177.

27 The Coptic uses the imperfect tense, and I have translated it as 'began to'.

the father of the mountain of Scetis[28]. The angel of the Lord spoke with the holy Apa Samuel, saying, "I myself know a great *anchorite*, he being *like* an *angel* on earth, (but) belonging to the heavenly Jerusalem, and his name is written in the Book of Life[29]. *So*, if you wish to become a *monk* and acquire the same *blessings* as him, then come and I shall give you to him, and you will become a *monk* with him." The holy Apa Samuel *prostrated himself*[30] before the angel, saying, "I beg you, my brother, do good to me as you wish."

He spent a long time stretched out before him on the ground until the *angel* took his hand, raising him up and saying, "Arise, young man. The wealth of your parents has prevailed in heaven[31]. Silas and Kosmiane have preceded you to the kingdom of heaven. *So*, have courage, my son Samuel, and do not allow the *desire* of this *world* to overcome you so that you estrange yourself from the great glory which your father has received in the kingdom of heaven. Therefore, keep your *body* pure from all defilement, and God will be with you and His *angels* will be your companions." When the *angel* had said this to him, he said to him, "Follow me." *Then* he went before him and brought him to a great high peak between Apa Macarius and Apa John2[32]. The angel of the Lord stretched out his hand to the holy Apa Samuel, saying, "Look, the *cave* of Apa Agathou, next to a rocky peak. Go in to him in *peace* and he will receive you in joy. Obey him in everything he will say to you and imitate his *life* and good example and follow him in everything." When the *angel* of the Lord had said this to him, he disappeared.

---

28 The monastery of Macarius (mod.Deir Abu Maqar) was founded in the second half of the 4th cent, cf.Evelyn-White *Hist*. 106.

29 cf. Phil.4, 3.

30 By the early Christian period the term had come to mean not only repentance, but also the act of it i.e. prostration; the Coptic illustrates this rather neatly.

31 This must refer to their 'spiritual' wealth cf.Matt. 19, 21.

32 E-White *Hist*. 252 n.5 says that this refers perhaps to one of the 'knolls' in the area, which are 15-20m high.

The *angel* of the Lord hastened and went in to Apa Agathou and said to him, "When this young man, Samuel, comes to you today, receive him in joy, for he will be a great *perfect one* of God[33]. Pray over him and clothe him with the habit of monkhood[34]. The Lord will bless the memory of his *monkhood*, and his name will endure for all the *generations* of the world. This one will be a *noble* son and a staff in your old age[35]. Instruct him and teach him about the things which you do, and instruct him in all the rules of *monkhood*. And his name is Samuel[36]." When the angel *had* said this to the old man, he disappeared. At that moment the holy Apa Samuel knocked at the door of the holy Apa Agathou[37].

5.   THE OLD MAN OPENED THE DOOR AND RECEIVED HIM IN great joy, saying, "Welcome, Samuel my son. God has sent you to me that you may *minister* to me in my old age." And he prayed over the hair tunic and the *cowl* and the holy *habit* saying, God of my holy fathers, Apa Macarius and Apa Antony, will be with you, Samuel my son, and He will bear with you in all

---

33   It is tempting to think that this is a 'technical' phrase referring to a certain stage of a monk's career and corresponding to the meaning "fully instructed" given by Lampe *Pat.Gk. Lexicon* 1381 F (though there is no ex. of its being applied to monks). It is perhaps worth noting that Samuel, on his deathbed, declares that "over sixty brothers have kept all the commandments" (p.117), although there were a hundred and twenty monks in the monastery (p.118).

34   The "schema" was *the* garment of monasticism; for a description of monastic initiation cf. E-White *Hist.*p.191if. Though the earliest known text of the rite is from the 14th cent., it seems likely (if only *a priori*) that the ceremony was established much earlier than this.cf. Evetts "Rite" *ROC* 11, 60ff.

35   The image of the son as the staff of his father's old is common in Pharaonic tomb inscriptions, where it is used as a title: *mdw i3w* cf. *Aeg.Wb.* II 178; for a discussion of the term
cf. Griffith *Hieratic Papyri* (text) 30.

36   And translates . It appears to be used by way of general explanation, and I have avoided for on the grounds that this would imply a logical nexus between the two statements, which is hardly likely.

37   The door of this cave was probably a makeshift affair; perhaps it was no more than a curtain.

your tribulations." He instructed him in humility and humble expression and *seemliness* and how to say at all times, "Forgive me. Please make me humble." Apa Samuel *prostrated himself* before Apa Agathou on his hands and feet, saying, "Remember me, my lord father, that God may forgive me my sins and enable me to do His will." And the holy Apa Samuel *strove* to imitate his father Apa Agathou in everything, *whether* it was *faith or ascetic practice or* mercy, while making two day fasts at all times, *or* his movements full of *seemliness or* the manner of his loving God *or* his endurance at prayer and his standing in fear and trembling[38].

The holy Apa Samuel progressed daily in his *monkhood*, the Holy *Spirit* helping him in everything he tried, while he *prostrated himself* before his father Apa Agathou at all times, kissing him on his hands and feet as he spoke with him in the word of God. He looked to his words as a field looks to its sower that he may sow in it good *fruit*, and as a vineyard waits for its gardener to *prune* it. Such was the way of Samuel as he looked to the word of God at all times[39].

6.   *THEN* AFTER THREE YEARS, AS APA AGATHOU ENDURED his many *ascetic practices* with Apa Samuel, *then* the Lord visited Apa Agathou: he took to his bed and was ill, and so he spent three months lying ill in bed, while Apa Samuel *attended* him in fear of God and *spiritual love*, taking care of him in every way appropriate to his illness. Afterwards Apa Agathou went to his rest, and his *spirit* was redoubled upon Apa Samuel his son and his *disciple*, like Elijah and Elisha, and he *inherited* eternity[40].

After the death of his *spiritual* father, the holy Apa Samuel increased his *ascetic practices* and *habits*[41]. He would make two

---

38 cf.Eph.6, 5.

39 This is similar to a sentiment expressed in a letter published by Till Gramm.316.

40 cf. II Kings 2, 9ff.

41 This phrase contains the Gk words and the first is particular, the second general.

day fasts, and when the *Sunday* of Lent arrived, he would not eat food until the *Saturday* of Easter[42], *except* for mountain *herbs* and raw vegetables: and he continued in this manner until his old age, God having *granted* him a *spiritual love* and *discernment* towards all brothers, being to them like a father and teacher and guide to *virtue*. They *believed in* his words like an *angel* of God, all looking to the *purpose* of his *life* and his *spiritual conversation*, as he was to them all like a *pillar* of light in the entire mountain of Scetis[43].

All the brothers who were disturbed and whose *bodily passions* *bothered* them at night and in the day, whenever they came to him that he might talk to them and they saw his good example and the honour of his *virginity* shining upon his face, they felt a great comfort and *spiritual* joy, for a *spirit* of God was in him, *working* its healing gift, so that his fame reached the north of the country, *almost* the *cities* on the coast[44], *so that* the sick and those with *unclean spirits* were brought to him. And when he prayed over them, God *granted* them a cure; and when the *merchants* who *sail* on the *sea* were overtaken by *danger*, the moment they uttered only his name, "God of Apa Samuel, *help* us", God saved them and their *merchandise*.[45]

7.   LET US *THEN* LEAVE BEHIND US THE *PROEMIUM* AND TURN to the *story* which lies before us and his departure from Scetis and let us tell you why he left the mountain of Scetis and came to the province of the Fayyum and how, by divine *providence*[46], he came and settled in the mountain of Kalamun.

---

42   The Coptic terms for these are lit. 'binding' and 'loosening'
43   For this phrase cf. also J.Barns in *JTS* 1960 p.73.
44   I think that here has the sense given by Liddell and Scott *Gk-Eng.Lexicon* 1744a: "used to soften a positive assertion with a sense of modesty"; cf.82, 39.
45   There are two quotations from Acts in this passage: 5, 16 and 2, 21.
46   'Divine providence' is a fundamental element of this story.

It happened at the time of Cyrus the *criminal*[47], when he came to the *city* of Alexandria[48] *in pursuit* of the holy *archbishop* Apa Benjamin[49]. He sought after him with false charges with the intention of killing him and sitting on his *throne, but* our God the *Christ* Jesus, who knows about everything before it happens, *then* saved the *archbishop* from the hands of the *impious one*; He hid him in the south of Egypt.

After this the *Colchian*[50] sat on the throne and he was given *civil authority*[51]. *Then* when he sat on the *throne tyrannically*, he issued the *Tome* of Leo[52]. Later he sent a cruel *magistrianus*[53] into the holy mountain of Scetis, his feet hastening to shed blood[54]. He gave him the polluted *Tome* of Chalcedon and told him[55], saying, "Let all the elders *subscribe* to this *Tome* from the smallest

---

47 Cyrus had been Bishop of Phasis, on the Black Sea coast in the Caucasus, hence his nickname the 'Colchian' or 'Caucasian'. He was appointed to the See of Alexandria by the Emperor Heraclius in 631 cf. Frend *Rise* 349-351. One might legitimately speculate that Heraclius wanted a forceful as well as reliable Chalcedonian Patriarch in Alexandria, who would not hesitate to use force if necessary. Whether Cyrus resorted to force of his own accord or on instructions from the Emperor is not known.

48 The Copts always referred to Alexandria by its Egyptian name 'Rakote'.

49 Benjamin was the Monophysite Patriarch from 623 to 665. For a detailed account of his career cf. Müller "Benjamin I, Patriarch von Alexandrien" *Muséon* 59, 313-340.

50 Cyrus is referred to only twice by his proper name in this text; otherwise he is called the 'Colchian'. This name went into Arabic as 'Muqauqis'.

51 Cyrus was not the first Patriarch to have civil and ecclesiastical authority: both had been held by Paul of Tabennese under Justinian cf. J.Maspero *Hist. Pat.*45. The granting of such absolute power may indicate the Emperor's anxiety to see Egypt reconciled to orthodoxy and the Empire.

52 An anachronistic reference to the new Monothelite or Monergist doctrine with which Heraclius hoped to end the schism that had existed in the oriental Christian world since 451. In the view of the Monophysite Egyptians it was the Tome of Leo which had caused this schism by insisting on the two natures of Christ. For a discussion of the Monothelite doctrine cf. Frend *Rise* 346-349.

53 'Magistrianus' means an agent of some sort, perhaps with imperial status.

54 cf.Rom.3, 15.

55 The Coptic has lit. 'But let all. . .' Is something missing?

to the greatest, because it was on those elders that the entire *country* of Egypt depended[56]. And exercise your zeal in searching the cells of the monks and the deserts. *In particular* you will find the one with the great beard[57] and send him to me that I may take my revenge on him; for while he *still* lives, my kingdom and *archbishopric* do not extend throughout the entire *country* of Egypt[58]."

And so the *magistrianus* came to Scetis with great pomp[59], two hundred soldiers following him, and occupied the great *church* of Apa Macarius[60]. He *ordered* them to assemble all the elders from the smallest to the greatest. He sought after the *hegumen* of Scetis, who was called John; but they did not find him, because all the possessions of the *church* were in his keeping, and for this reason he fled to the inner *marsh*. *Berbers* saw him there and took him *prisoner* to their own country[61]. *Then* when the *magistrianus* had assembled all the brothers, he caused the polluted *Tome* of Leo to be read out to them. He also caused a *letter* of the *Colchian* to be read out to them[62], *teaching* them with his *misleading* words and urging them on to the *Tome* which was full of darkness. *Then* after the reading of the *letter*, he caused a *deacon* to raise his

56   I have tried to translate here a Coptic 'second' tense, which usually emphasises an adverbial phrase.

57   Benjamin's beard is also mentioned in the "Apocalypse of Samuel" cf. Ziadeh *ROC* 20, 393.

58   Müller points out in his article (326) that Benjamin's was a well-planned flight, during which he was still able to issue instructions and thereby exercise considerable influence.

59   Used in a derogatory sense. Significantly the term is used also of the renegade Bishop of the Fayyum (83, 24) and the devil (112, 46), though I am not certain of the precise translation in the latter case.

60   The 'great church' was probably destroyed during the Berber attack on Scetis in 570; it is not known if it was rebuilt. It is possible that the phrase 'these lifeless stones' (to which the magistrianus points cf.80, 31) may refer to rubble.

61   John was eventually taken to the Oasis of Siwa, where Samuel met him some years later cf.p.91ff.

62   The new doctrine had presumably been translated into Coptic.

voice in the crowd, saying, "My holy fathers, do you *believe* thus *according* to that which is written in this *Tome*?" But they were silent. *Again* he spoke, as many as three times, *but* they made no reply.

The *magistrianus* became very angry and ordered them to be flogged, saying, "Why have you nothing to say, but remain silent like these *lifeless* stones? And why have you not given me your blessing and said *'Welcome*, you and your king who sent you'? Perhaps you think I shall refrain from shedding your blood. No! *Heaven forbid*! I shall not spare you in any way!" *Then* he said, "Will you still not speak, infuriating *monks*?" And at that moment the holy Apa Samuel leaped up, ready to give his *life* to death and to show fortitude. He said to the magistrianus,"What do you want us to do for you? We do not accept this *Tome* or that which is written in it, *nor* yet do we accept the *Council* of Chalcedon *nor* do we have any *archbishop* but our father Apa Benjamin."

After this the magistrianus became angry and ground his teeth at Samuel. He said to him, "By the *power* of kings[63], I shall make you *subscribe* to this Tome first and you will *confess* all the things in it, because you have acted shamelessly and spoken *evilly*." The holy Apa Samuel prepared himself to give his life to death. He said to the *magistrianus*,"This is a mere trifle which you have adjured me to perform. Bring the *Tome* here to me, and I shall convince you." The *magistrianus*, overjoyed, caused it to be given to him. When it was placed in his hand, Samuel held it out towards the people, saying, "My fathers, do you accept this *Tome*? *Anathema* to this *Tome*. *Anathema* to the *Council* of Chalcedon. *Anathema* to the *impious* Leo. *Anathema* to everyone who believes according to it."

---

63 It was customary to swear by the of the Emperor, but is used in an oath of the 8th cent. cf. Crum and Steindorff *Koptische Rechtsurkunden* 74.

He hastily tore up the *Tome* and threw it outside the door of the *church*. The *magistrianus* was filled with *anger* against the holy Apa Samuel; he snorted through his nose and forced his hands together[64]. He caused ten soldiers to flog him at once, until everyone said that he was already dead. The *magistrianus* was urging them on against him, "Flog him with raw-hide *thongs.*" After this he made them bind his hands behind his back, tie a rope to one of his feet and suspend him. Then they fixed him on stakes and *tortured* him until his blood flowed like water[65]. A thong which an *attendant* held slipped from his hand and fell on his right eye[66], whereupon his pupil immediately burst and spilled down upon his cheek. When the *magistrianus* saw that his eye had been displaced and that his blood was flowing like water, he immediately *returned to his senses* and abated a little in his anger. He made the soldiers stop flogging him and said to the holy one, "Your eye which has been displaced has saved you from death, *admirable monk*[67]." He made twelve soldiers *drive* him and his *monastic* children *out* and throw him off the mountain of Scetis.

8.   AS TO WHAT HAPPENED *THEN* IN SCETIS, WE SHALL BE silent,[68] and we shall turn to the holy *champion* Apa Samuel and reveal the prize of his faith. When the soldiers *pursued* him out of Scetis until they drove him south from the mountain, himself and his few *disciples*, his *disciples* supporting him on either side,

---

64   'Snorting through the nose' is an activity associated with the devil cf.Drescher *Mus*.82, 90; I am not certain what he was doing with his hands: wringing them perhaps?

65   A commonplace in martyrological texts.

66   There is a portrait of Samuel with one eye in Meinardus *Monks* 311, though it is his left eye which is missing there.

67   'Admirable' is a conjectural translation: the Coptic reads , and I think it may be a corruption of , a term used in Classical Greek in an ironical way.

68   Evelyn-White takes this to mean that many of the monks cpaitulated c f. *Hist.* 256', however, it may mean simply that the author wishes to transfer the scene of the action from Scetis.

since he was very *weak*, they accompanied him[69] south from Scetis in great pain and distress, until they reached a small *cave* perched in the mountain, and they laid him out on the mountain, like a corpse gasping in a deathly fashion. His *disciples* wept over him, saying, "Woe to us, our father. Soon you will be dead."

And they hastily dug a hole to bury his *body*, but in the middle of the night an *angel* of the Lord descended from heaven and stood in the middle of the *cave*, burning like a fiery flame. His *disciples* were afraid and fainted from fear. The *angel* of the Lord took the hand of Apa Samuel and raised him, "Do not be afraid, holy one. The Lord has sent me to you that I may give you strength'.' And he laid his hand upon his face, and immediately he was able to see; he laid his hand upon the whole of his *body*, and immediately he was healed; *rather* even greater strength came to him. The *angel* said to him, "Arise and go south to the province of the Fayyum, and dwell in a *monastery* called Neklone[70]. Behold, one crown you have received[71], because you have fought for the *faith* of your fathers; another two crowns await you, one in the Fayyum, one in another country far away; and thereafter honour will be yours and the memory of your name will endure through all the *generations* of the earth."

When the *angel* had said this to him, he went up to heaven in glory, the holy man looking after him[72]. The holy Apa

---

69 I am not certain about the translation here. I have rendered this as though it were part of a main clause, but there is room for doubt in the Coptic, which uses a circumstantial tense (often translated by English participle). Some confusion also arises from the fact that verb which I translate here as 'accompany' occurs two lines earlier and means 'lead forth' or 'drive out' and is used of the soldiers.

70 The monastery of Neklone seems to have been established in the 4th cent, and declined as Kalamun flourished cf.102, 23ff. where the transfer of monks to Kalamun is described. It was c.10km south of Medinet el-Fayyum cf. Abbott *Mon.Fayyum* 28ff.

71 The three crowns of martyrdom are a commonplace in Coptic literature cf. Hyvernat *Martyres* I 261.

72 cf.Acts 1, 10.

Samuel hastily aroused his *disciples*, Jacob, Joseph, Solomon and Selbane[73]. They proceeded south to the province of the Fayyum, walking along and singing this *psalm*, "Our[74] life is saved like a sparrow from the hand of the hunter; the trap is broken, and we are saved. We have *help* from the name of the Lord, who created heaven and earth." *So then*, they came down to the province of the Fayyum and settled in the holy *monastery* of Neklone. The holy Apa Samuel, together with his sons, was attentive to his *prayers*[75], as they continued in *psalms* and *songs* and prayers and manual labour and nights of vigil. He was in great calm and *peace*, as they went in humility of heart and good conduct, *submitting* to both small and great in all gentleness. And they *strove* to perform all good works (and to show) *piety*, purity and *righteousness*; and they were servants of God, and God Himself looked after them everywhere, because they were His servants.

All the brothers who lived in the mountain of Neklone, when they saw their *attitude* and good example, thanked God, saying, "Our *monastery* has been considered worthy of a great honour, for this saintly man has settled in it with his *spiritual* children." Then the scripture was fulfilled[76], "Let your good works be seen and let glory be given to your Father Who is in heaven." So they felt great *faith* in the holy Apa Samuel as they saw him praying over the brothers who were sick, and the received healing from him. After he had been some days in the mountain of Neklone, the fame of his sweet odour went from the Fayyum and *almost* reached the neighbouring districts, and everyone who was sick with any disease was brought to him, and the Lord *granted* healing to them through him. *For* God the *Christ* was revealing His saints, giving glory to them everywhere and not allowing

---

73 For Silvanus?

74 cf. Ps.124, 7-8.

75 Translates . H. Quecke discusses the use of the verb and the noun in Coptic: broadly speaking the vb. Means 'celebrate the Mass', while the nn. can mean either 'Mass' or 'prayer' cf. *Kopt. Stundengebet* 118-123.

76 cf. Matt.5, 16.

them to be hidden, *even as* He has said with His divine mouth, "You are the light of the *world*. It is impossible for a *city* to remain concealed if it is built on a mountain, nor is a lamp lit and placed under a bushel, *but* it is put on the *lampstand* that it may give light to those who are in the house."[77]

9.   WHEN THE HOLY APA SAMUEL SAW THAT MEN TROUBLED him very much and that they did not let him alone for a single day, he made for himself a *cave* on the east side of the *monastery*, about a *mile* away, and nobody knew of it. The holy Apa Samuel would shut himself up in it for the whole *week* working on nets, which are called baskets[78]. When he reached *Saturday* and *Sunday*, he would go to the *monastery* to *celebrate the mass* and he would find a crowd of people assembled at the outer *gate*, where his small cell[79] was, many among them sick or troubled. The holy Apa Samuel, because of his great philanthropy and mercy, would pray over them all and *make sign of the cross* over them, and their health would be restored to them all immediately; and they would return home, rejoicing and giving glory to God and the holy Apa Samuel.

Then after Samuel had spent a full year in complete peace in the small *cave*, Cyrus the *Colchian* came south from the land of Egypt, *conducting the persecution* everywhere and seeking after the holy Apa Benjamin. Every *monk* he came upon, he would make him *subscribe* to the defiled *Tome* of the *impious* Leo and *celebrate the mass* with him. After this he came into the province of the Fayyum with great *pomp*, and Victor the *Bishop* of the Fayyum[80] came out to meet him in great joy and empty glory of

---

77 cf. Matt.5, 14; for the variant reading 'built on a mountain' cf. Kuhn in Muséon 73,319ff.

78 The Coptic word is intended to explain the Gk. ; does this mean that there were certain types of basket commonly called 'nets' because of a particular type of weaving which resembled that found in nets.

79 The gate of the monastery must have been a fairly noisy place; was it awarded to Samuel because he was a comparative newcomer?

80 Victor is reviled in Monophysite literature as a traitor cf. Mliller *Homilie* 84.

this *world*, glory being given to him until he was received into the *city* of the Fayyum. After this he issued forth from the city of the Fayyum the polluted *Tome* of Chalcedon, by the *order* of Justinian the *false*-king of the *Romans*[81], who *ordered* that the entire *land* of Egypt should *be a party to* the defiled Tome of Chalcedon. When the *orthodox people* saw that the *Colchian* had begun to *lead* them *astray* with his *erroneous* words, they *retired* each to his own place and left him, so as to ignore him.

When the *Colchian* saw that the *magistrates* and the rest of the *orthodox* avoided and ignored him and did not obey his *erroneous* words, he then became very angry and said to himself, "I shall arise and visit the *monasteries* of the entire district, and I shall make the *monasteries* submit to me and the *monks* first *subscribe* to the *Tome* of *Leo* and my *faith*: if they *subscribe*, then the *people* will *subscribe* without any *hesitation*[82]." He went forth into all the *monasteries*, and the *monks* he found, he caused them to *subscribe* to the *Tome* of Chalcedon and *celebrate the mass* with him.

Then the holy Apa Samuel, when he saw the great destruction which had been wrought by the *deceitful Colchian*, assembled all the brothers who were on the mountain of Neklone: they numbered two hundred *lay* brothers[83] and one hundred and twenty *monks*. He spent a long time talking to them in the word of God, teaching them what was good for their *souls* and speaking with them in words of entreaty, saying, "I *call upon* you, my brothers and my fathers, that each of you may conceal himself wherever he pleases for a few days, until the Lord Jesus delivers us and saves us from this foul *subscription* and the vile

---

81 Justinian died in 567, but his name may have been especially loathsome to the Monophysites since it was he who reintroduced the succession of Chalcedonian Patriarchs in Alexandria. The Emperor at this period was Heraclius.

82 Cyrus was probably right to have such faith in the influence of the monks.

83 I have not been able to find any parallel usage of this term in Coptic. Evelyn-White speaks of 'lay monks of acknowledged eminence' {History 171,176), but seems to assume their existence rather than substantiate it.

blasphemies of the polluted *Council* of Chalcedon, and I *believe* that if you listen to me, God will guide us and save us and *protect* your dwelling places, and He will return you to your *monasteries* in *peace*, without any harm." When the holy Apa Samuel said this, this words pleased all the brothers; they left him, saying, "Bless us, our holy father. We are prepared to die for the *upright faith*." The holy Apa Samuel blessed them and sent them away in *peace*, he *retired* with his disciples.

10.   THEN WHEN MORNING CAME AND THE SUN WAS JUST rising, three soldiers came to the *monastery* to prepare the place for the arrival of the *Colchian*. They did not find a single *monk*, except only the one who *serves*. The soldiers hastily seized him, took him with them and *met* the *Colchian* on the road at the mouth of the canal[84]. They said to him, "We did not find a *monk* in the entire monastery apart from this one." The *Colchian* said to him, "Why have the *monks* not come out to meet me? For what *reason* have they gone away?" The *steward*[85] said, "I do not know why they have gone.'

He *ordered* him to be flogged until he told him everything that had taken place. The *steward* said, "Do not flog me. I will tell you the truth. For this man Samuel, the *ascete*, gave a long *harangue*, reproving them[86] in his speech and calling you a blasphemer (and saying that) you were a godless Chalcedonian Jew and that we were not to *celebrate the mass* with you or *communicate* with you in any way. Therefore the *monks* obeyed him and all retired." When the *Colchian* heard this, he became very angry: he chewed his lips in a furious rage and cursed the *steward* and the *monastery* and the *monks* who lived in it. He turned to another road, and he has not been up to the mountain to this day.

---

84 The canal may refer to Illahun c.10km NE of Neklone; the Arabic name is based on the Coptic word for 'canal'.

85 The steward was usually in charge of the stores; he may have been left behind to take care of these in the temporary absence of the monks.

86 Codex B reads "you", which makes better sense.

11.   AFTER THIS THE BROTHERS RETURNED TO THE *MONASTERY*
in peace. The *false-archbishop* was wicked enough to go to the city
of the Fayyum; immediately he sent servants and acquaintances[87]
to go to the mountain of Neklone and bring to him Apa Samuel,
his hands tied behind his back and a *chain* on his neck. *And so*
they came to the *monastery* and found the holy man. They seized
him and took him to Cyrus. As he was walking along, rejoicing
in the *spirit*, he was saying, "May it happen that my blood will
be shed today for the name of the Lord Jesus *Christ*." Thus he
insulted the *Colchian* before everyone, so that perhaps he might
kill him. Whereupon the Colchian told his soldiers, "Bring me
this unholy *monk*." *And so* the soldiers *brought* him before Cyrus.

When the *impious* one saw the man of God, he was filled with
rage against him and *ordered* the soldiers to flog him until his
blood flowed like water. He then said to him, "Are you Samuel,
the iniquitous ascete? Who *appointed* you *hegumen* over this
monastery? Who ordered you to teach the *monks* to defect from
me and my *faith*?" The holy Apa Samuel replied, "It is better to
obey God and our father, the *archbishop* Benjamin, than to obey
you and your *demonic* teaching, you son of Satan and *deceiving
Antichrist*." When the *Colchian* heard this, he ordered that
Samuel be struck on the mouth, crying out and saying, "Samuel,
the praise that men give you has destroyed your *mind*. But I shall
chastise you and teach to speak *properly*[88]; for this reason[89] you
have not honoured me *as archbishop nor* have you honoured my
authority as *civil ruler*[90] of the *land* of Egypt."

---

87 These were presumably men he could trust.

88 Codex B reads "badly", which I think is perhaps better: the sense would be 'I
will teach you about speaking badly'.

89 I think that this phrase refers to Samuel's 'speaking badly', which in Cyrus'
view has caused him to ignore these courtesies.

90 The Greek word denotes a military rank 'squadron commander' or 'captain'.

The holy Apa Samuel answered, saying to the *Colchian*, "Mastema too is a ruler[91]: he rules the *angels*, his arrogance and faithlessness having estranged from God and His *angels*. But you, Chalcedonian *heretic*, your faith is defiled and you are more accursed than the *devil* and his *demons*." When the *Colchian* heard this, he became extremely angry and he signalled to the soldiers to beat him to death. *In a word* he began to kill[92] the *righteous* man, except that the *magistrates* of the *city* of Fayyum saved Samuel from him. When he saw that he had escaped from his hands, he ordered that Samuel be cast out from the mountain of Neklone, saying, "If you will not *communicate* with me in my *faith*, retire from the *monasteries* of this province, lest you perish *miserably* at my hands."

12.   IT HAPPENED AFTER THIS THAT WHILE SAMUEL WAS *STILL* weak, behold an *angel* of the Lord came to him and healed all his wounds. He said to him, "Arise and go south to the mountain of Takinash[93] and settle there with your *disciples*." And so he left the mountain of Neklone with his *disciples* and travelled south, singing *psalms* and saying, "With the help of my God I shall pass through a wall[94]" and "Who is God but our Lord God Who girds me with strength, You Who have made my way holy[95]?" *Then* after this he went to the mountain of Takinash and settled in it with his children in complete quiet and calm, making many prayers and *fasts*, *meditations* and ceaseless nights of vigil.

At all times he said, "Prayer and *fasting* are the redemption of the soul[96]. Prayer and *fasting* are the perfume of the *angels*. Prayer

---

91   A name of the devil which first occurs in the Bk. of Jubilees cf. R.Charles *Apocrypha* c.10, 8ff.

92   The Coptic uses a preposition with this verb, which has the effect of emphasising the proposed activity.

93   For a discussion of the location of Takinash cf. Daressy in *Ann.Serv.* 18, 26-28.

94   cf. Ps.18, 29.

95   cf. Ps.18, 32.

96   Occurs later on in the second 'litany' to prayer and fasting cf.105, 23.

and *fasting* are the *denunciation* of the sin. Prayer and *fasting* are the purity of the saints. Prayer and *fasting* are the *practices* of the *angels*. It is prayer and *fasting* which *drive* out the *demons*. It was prayer and *fasting* which caused Moses to speak with God[97]. Through prayer and *fasting* Elijah and Elisha walked upon the waters of the Jordan[98]. Through prayer and *fasting* Paul was saved[99] in the *sea* voyage. Let everyone who wishes to become a *monk* love prayer and *fasting*. Without prayer and *fasting* the *monk* does not escape the *passions* of the *devil.*"

And *then* after this *just* as the God of Glory appeared to our father Abraham, when he was in Mesopotamia, before he settled in the land of Haran, saying, "Come forth from your land and *family*, and come to the land which I shall show you[100]", so also He appeared to our father Apa Samuel while he was *still* dwelling in the mountain of Takinash, before he settled in the *marsh*[101], saying to him, "Come forth from this place and leave behind your *disciples* and come to the wilderness which I shall show." The holy Apa Samuel hastened to reply to the voice of the Lord Sabaoth and said, "I, your servant, am ready, behold, to follow you." He *then* made an *agreement* with his *disciples*, saying, "Behold, I shall go into this desert and not return to you for many days, *but* look for me at the holy *Pasch* of the Lord. If I come back to you, you will see me, but if not, do not come into the desert *on* any account looking for me, my beloved children." After this he arose with his children and prayed with them, leaving them on the sixteenth day of Mesore, which is the day of the *assumption* of Our Lady the holy *God-Bearer*, Mary[102].

---

97   cf. Ex.3, 4.

98   cf. II Kings 2, 8.

99   cf. Acts c.27.

100   cf. Gen. 12, 1.

101   For a geographical description of this 'marsh' cf. Azadian, Hug and Munier in *Bull.Soc.Roy.GSog.Egypte* 18, 47-63.

102   August 9.

So he made his way into the mountains; the saint walked, without knowing where he was going, like Abraham at the time when he came forth, walking without knowing where he was going, *but believing* in God that He has power in all things. So the holy Apa Samuel was firm in his resolve as he made his way into the mountain. *In fact,* he girded himself with the *armour* of God and a powerful *faith*[103], having set off into the mountain with a single purpose, and he walked until he came to the *marsh*. He looked down into it and saw many date palms in it and a small *church*[104]. So he stood praying and saying, "*Almighty* Lord God, may You hear my prayer and listen to my plea in Your truth[105]. For You are the One Who revealed Himself to our father Abraham. You promised Isaac to him. Then You said to Jacob[106], You shall not be called Jacob, *but* Israel shall be your name". And he said, 'I have seen God face to face, and my *soul* has been preserved[107].' Now, my Lord, tell me what I must do."

While he was *still* praying, he heard a voice saying, "Samuel, Samuel, I have heard your plea and your prayer. Your voice has come unto me. *Now* take courage and fear not. I am with you. Behold I shall give this land as an *inheritance* to you and your children who shall come after you for a glory *beyond* that of the saints. And I Myself am with My saints who shall come after you." And he ceased to hear the voice.

13.   *Then* he went down into the *marsh*, singing *psalms* in great joy. Thereupon an *angel* appeared to him in great glory. When the holy man saw him, he was afraid and fell on his face upon the ground. The *angel* gave him his hand and raised him

---

103   cf. Eph.6, 13.

104   There had been a community at Kalamun in the 5th cent, cf. Abbott *Mon. Fayyum* 35.

105   cf. Ps.143, 1.

106   I believe this passage to be corrupt; my translation is based on an emended version cf. n.128 (text).

107   cf. Gen.32, 30.

up, and he said to him, "Do not be afraid. The Lord is with you. This is the land which the Lord has promised to you and your *seed* forever. Instead of the consolation of children *after the flesh* God will grant you *righteous* elders[108]" The *angel* took his hand and led him into the small *church*. He said to him, "Take courage and be strong. The Lord is with you." And the *angel* disappeared. The old man prayed thus, "I shall go into Your house and worship Your holy temple." *Then* he found the small *church* covered in sand, for it had long been uninhabited[109]. *And so* he spent a long time and many days until he had *cleaned* it *thoroughly*. The saint sat down in the *church*, among great prayers and entreaties, giving glory to God, because He had prepared for him such a home in the desert. He took his small *sustenance* from the fruit of the date palms that were there. After this the devil appeared to our father, Apa Samuel, *threatening*[110] him, "This is an outrage! I have left aside for you the world, *monk*, but it has not been sufficient for you, so that you 35 come to the place where I live with those who belong to me[111]. *To be sure*, are you following the example of this one called Antony? If so, I shall fight with you too." Thereupon he spread his hands out, saying, "Lord You are my light and my *saviour*. Whom shall I fear?" And the *devil* disappeared.

---

108   Inability to have one's own children must have been one of the most painful aspects of monasticism for Egyptians, for they have always (like most Mediterranean peoples) been very attached to their families; not surprisingly therefore the citizen of the heavenly Jerusalem will instead be father to more spiritual children.

109   The church had probably been uninhabited since the 5th cent. With the constant threat of Berber raids, especially with its desolate location, Kalamun would have attracted only the most courageous.

110   Drescher discusses this term in *Muséon* 85, 290 and 89, 308.

111   A similar exchange between Samuel and the devil takes place later on cf. 112, 35.

14.   SOME DAYS LATER *BERBERS*[112] DESCENDED ON THE *MARSH* from the west. When the saint looked and saw them, he was very troubled. He sought to conceal himself from them, *but* God did not *grant* that this should happen *without* trouble, so that the *endurance* of the *righteous one* should be evident, together with his *faith*. *Then* the holy Apa Samuel heard a voice saying, "Samuel, Samuel, fear not. Get yourself into the *church* and remain there. Do not speak. I shall not let them see you." He went and did as he was told. Thereupon the *Berbers* went into the *church*, with their swords drawn in their hands and shouting in their language[113]. When the saint saw them in this way, he became very frightened and trembled as he saw their *audacious treatment* of the *church* and *altar*.

He responded (to this) and said, "What are you doing, defiled and *impious* ones? The Lord God will repay you for this." The *Berbers* said to the saint, "How is it *then* that you have been sitting here and we have not seen you?" Thereupon they seized him and said to him, "Where are the *vessels*[114] that are in this place?" He told them, "There are no *vessels* in this place." They *attacked* him brutally. O God-loving *people*, see the wonders of God and His great philanthropy towards us. It was He Who said to the saint, "Do not speak", and yet it was He Who *granted* that he should speak, as I have already said[115]. The *Berbers* dragged him here and there, searching after the *vessels* of the *church*. They

---

112   Egypt had always suffered from the marauding inhabitants of the Western Desert; for an account of their depredations in the Christian period cf. Evelyn-White *Hist.*151ff. Outlying monasteries were easy prey, and there was doubtless a decent income to be got from valuable church property and the sale of monks as slaves.

113   Raised voices in a foreign language tend to be doubly frightening: they not only threaten, but they threaten the unknown. Samuel's behaviour is accordingly all the more courageous.

114   These would normally have been bronze or silver.

115   This seems an odd phrase, since it is only a few lines earlier that he actually did say it and it seems unlikely that anyone would have forgotten.

then bound him to a column[116] of the *church* with great cruelty and inflicted upon him great blows, so that he was *in danger* of dying[117]. When they were exhausted from beating him and found out nothing from him, they threw him outside.

When they had thrown him out, the saint fell upon the ground and was unable to stand because of the many great blows they had inflicted upon him. They seized him by the foot and dragged him along pitilessly, until they brought him to the place where the camels were, others following him and beating him on the head and sides, *according* as our fathers have testified to us that the holy Apa Samuel *confessed* that this is what the godless Berbers did to him[118]. They then mounted him on a she camel that they might take him *prisoner* to their *country*. After they had mounted him and escorted him into the mountain, the Lord sent His *angel* that he might be saved from their hands that day.

15.   THE *ANGEL* PRICKED THE SIDE OF THE CAMEL, AND SHE immediately raised her face up to the face of Samuel. God gave the camel a human voice[119] and she spoke and said to Apa Samuel, "Old man, why are you weeping and sad at heart?" He was silent for a while, stunned by the voice of the camel. He said to the camel, "I am in pain from the many blows which they have dealt me and because they are taking me to a *country* which I do not know." The camel said to the saint, "They did *well* to beat you. They have done nothing to you *beyond* what you deserve. For what you deserve they have done to you, because you disobeyed

---

116   A. Fakhry visited Kalamun in the 1940s and photographed two Corinthian capitals outside the entrance; it is difficult to be certain, but they could be 5th cent cf. *Ann.Serv.* 46 pi.XI.

117   Drescher discusses this phrase in *Muséon* 82, 89.

118   Isaac is at pains to emphasise the authority for his statements.

119   The camel is an instrument of Divine Providence; I know of only one other instance where an animal is gifted with human speech in the service of God, a fragment of a text relating to Cosmas (and Damian?) in B.M.Or.7561/129 (unpublished).

the voice of the Lord Your God, which said, 'Do not speak.' For this reason you deserve great *punishment*."

When the old man heard this from the camel, he wept bitterly, saying, "*Truly* I have sinned and I reproach myself alone, *but* it is possible for God to forgive me my disobedience, because I was unable to control myself when I saw the temerity with which these *Berbers* treated the *church*. I spoke, for *necessity* forced me to speak *against* my wish[120], and I disobeyed." While the holy Apa Samuel was *still* saying these things to the camel, the angel of the Lord seized the legs of the camel and *prevented* her from walking forwards *or* backwards; *but* she stood, bellowing *excessively* so that she broke the ropes that were on her neck. *Then* the *Berbers* came to her and beat her severely[121], and she was unable to move forwards *or* backwards, *but* she lay down, the saint mounted on her. They untied him and dismounted him from her. When he was dismounted, she started and stood up; then she leapt forward and *bounded*, spitting so that she touched the other camels (with her spittle). *But* if anyone is *scandalised* at this small miracle, let him remember first the ass which spoke to Balaam, the *prophet*, reproaching him for his faithlessness, as it is written in the Book of *Numbers*.[122]

Now therefore, my beloved, do not wonder *or be distressed or* yet be *insensitive* like the godless Jews[123] and do not be *distrustful* of these holy miracles, but be *trusting* and *believe* what is written in the holy Scripture. Once again[124], the saint was mounted on the camel for the second time, *but* she would not go forwards *or*

---

120 Samuel is confronted by a genuine dilemma: should he obey the word of God or should he do what he knows to be right?

121 Most Beduin peoples are very fond of their camels, and it requires something serious for them to beat their animals.

122 cf. Num.22, 22.

123 A similar sentiment is expressed by Athanasius in his anti-Arian speeches cf. Migne *PG* 26,520a: is this an echo?

124 A Greco-Coptic tautology lit. 'again again'.

backwards, although she received many heavy blows so that she cried out loudly. The owner of the camel became very angry with the holy Apa Samuel because of the blows being inflicted on his camel. He ran up to the saint angrily, seized him by his leg[125] and hurled him to the ground. He drew his sword and came at him as if to kill him, except that one of the *Berbers prevented* him, saying, "Do not lay your hand upon him. Let us leave him on this mountain, and he will die alone[126]." And so they abandoned him on the mountain, stretched out. They went, left him and *withdrew* to their own *country*.

16.   THE HOLY APA SAMUEL WAS UTTERLY EXHAUSTED FROM the way he had been thrown from the camel and the blows he had received. And he spent four days walking on the road until he reached the *church* in great pain. *But* through all this he was strong of heart and thankful to the Lord giving glory to Him and saying[127], "Who shall be able to separate us from the love of God? *Tribulation*, anguish *persecution*, *danger or* the sword? *According* as it is written, 'For Your sake we are killed all the day long, and we are reckoned as sheep for the slaughter, *but* in all these things we gain greater victory through Christ Jesus.'"

Then after all this Samuel remained in the alone, amid numerous prayers and *fastings*. He met nobody *nor* did he enquire after his *disciples*, but he was attending to the things that will happen at the end.

17.   A FEW DAYS LATER, THE *BERBERS* HAPPENED TO COME wandering in from the mountain, stealing everything from the villagers whom they would[128] find living in the districts at the

---

125   I am not certain if this means 'leg' or 'foot'; the latter is the usual meaning.

126   For the same suggestion made about Samuel by his enemies cf. 112, 20.

127   cf. Rom. 8, 35.

128   This translates the fut. tense, which is used perhaps in sense given by Till. *Kopt. Gr.* §307 "bei Schatzungen und Vermutungen". It is certainly more vivid than a past tense.

foot of the mountain and taking their men as *prisoners* besides[129].
Now by Divine *Providence* the men of the villages knew that the
Berbers were coming upon them, and they hastily took their wives
and children, fled, abandoned their houses and possessions and
saved their *lives* from *captivity* among the *Berbers*. While it was
evening, the *Berbers* went into the village and took everything
they found. They went up into the mountain and came upon the
marsh of Kalamun as they were returning to their *country*.[130] It
happened after this that the holy Apa Samuel was in the southern
meadow, pruning his few date palms.

While he was *still* working on them, he was surrounded by the
Berbers, who seized him and beat him severely. They then tied
his hands behind his back and began to drag him back and forth,
as they sought after his clothes and possessions, but they found
nothing on him, *except* for a few dates. The *Berbers* behaved like
wild animals to him, *for* they thought in their hearts that *surely*
there was some person *or objects* about which he had not told
them. So they dragged him angrily until they brought him to
the north of the *spring*, a little to the south of the church[131], and
tied him to a date palm and beat him hard. O how great were the
blows inflicted on him by those godless *Berbers*.

They broke off fresh branches of date palm full of thorns and
beat the holy Apa Samuel violently until his blood flowed like
water. *Then* when they were exhausted with beating and he said
nothing to them at all, they mounted him on a she-camel and
took him with them as their *prisoner* to their *country*. O how
many are the trials which the saints receive for the kingdom of
heaven so that they might *inherit* it and its *benefits*. *Then* after
this it happened when the godless *Berbers* had taken the holy

---

129   Presumably men fetched a better price than women.
130   They probably went via the Bahriyah Oasis SW of Kalamun.
131   The spring obviously produced enough water to enable the monks to
cultivate crops etc. so that they could be self-sufficient for two years cf.102, 22.

Apa Samuel to their *country*, they sold him as a slave to a great *Berber*.

18.   NOW BY DIVINE *PROVIDENCE* HE *CAME UPON* THE VILLAGE where John the *Hegumen* of Scetis was living in slavery also[132]. The saint was sent out to the field to tend the camels; and it happened that whenever he went into the field, he met the holy Apa John: and they were in the habit of walking together and speaking of the miracles of God, comforting each other in the troubles they had suffered, reciting many prayers and supplications and *psalms* and *spiritual songs*, giving *doxologies* of blessing to *Christ*, because God had made them worthy to *meet* each other in a strange and *idolatrous* country. Apa John said to Samuel, being about to instruct him, "Take care, for these *Berbers* will *surely force* you to worship the sun[133]. *But* be strong and do not obey them, *for* I was severely beaten for this: *for* it is the *custom* that whenever they see the sun come up, they turn their faces to the east and worship it, saying, 'Welcome, our lord the Sun, for you have given us light in the darkness of the night.' And again, when it comes to *but* a little before setting, they turn to the west and worship it saying, 'Our lord the Sun, will you go and leave us in the darkness of the night? Come *quickly* up and give us light. '*Now* this, my holy father, is the *custom* the *Berbers* practise daily."

And it happened later as Samuel was in the country of the Maxyes[134], the devil hardened the heart of the *Berber* against the holy Apa Samuel, and he continued to afflict him a lot with hard labour. He then took him on to the roof of his house at the time when the sun was about to rise and *forced* him, saying to

---

132   John was captured by the Berbers shortly after his departure from Scetis c.631; cf.6, *26*ff.

133   Attempts had been made during the reign of Justinian to Christianise the Siwans, but they were evidently not entirely successful.

134   Also known as 'Mazices'; for a discussion of the name cf. Evelyn-White *Hist.*151-153.

him, "Come and worship the Sun too, the god of the *Maxyes*."
But the holy Apa Samuel strengthened his heart with great *faith*
in God and said to the Berber, "I shall not obey you in this;
nor may it happen to me that I should worship the Sun." The
Berber became very angry and seized Apa Samuel. He put his
hand upon the head and neck of Apa Samuel, saying, "I shall
not let you go unless you worship the Sun who is the lord and I
see you with my own eyes." *But* the *righteous* one, strong in his
heart and *faith*, the blessed *confessor*, lifted up his neck from the
hand of the *Berber* with great strength and spat towards the sun,
saying, "May it never happen to me that I should worship the
sun, which God has put there to give light to the earth for the
service of man."

When the *servant* of the *Berber* saw this, he tore his clothes apart
and said to the *Berber*, the master of Samuel, "Do you not see
him spitting at our god?" The *Berber* said, "Why do you spit at
our lord the Sun? Do you wish him to be angry with us and not
come and leave our whole *country* in darkness because of you?"
Believe me, my brothers, that the *Berber* inflicted many blows on
the face of Apa Samuel and cast him to the ground many times,
with the intention of killing him; *but* God did not wish this to
happen, *but* He gave him strength to complete his *contest*. O the
one who became a *martyr* many times without losing his life!
O *confessor* and *athlete* of the *orthodox faith*! I beg and *entreat*
you, my holy father, that you may *entreat* God for myself and
everyone who hears me today, that He may forgive our sins and
help me to complete the rest of your *achievements* and the pains
which you suffered for the name of *Christ*.

Then after these great blows which that cruel *Berber* inflicted
upon him, he tied him to a thorn-tree[135], which was inside the
camel-pen, and left him there for five days without food and
water. He did not beat him again, *nor* did he *force* him to worship

---

135 Acacia nilotica.

the sun. *For* he was afraid *lest* he might spit at it again as before.
When John the *Hegumen* of Scetis saw the great cruelty of the
Berber towards the holy Apa Samuel, that he became very weak
and that the saint remained tied to the thorn, he was disturbed
and deeply saddened.

He went to the *Berber* who was his own master and *begged* him
to go to the *Berber* master of Samuel that he might release him.
He took two others with him and went to the *Berber*; and when
he asked him, he released the old man in an extremely weak
condition. He sent him to the fields to tend the camels; he spent
two *Weeks* lying ill in a hut, the holy Apa John *ministering* to
him, *for* many *weals* had formed on his *body* as a result of the
injuries inflicted on him by the *Berber*. *Then* after a few days
God took pity on him and caused the *wounds* on his *body* to heal.
The holy Apa Samuel recovered his strength completely; and he
and John were[136] in the fields, tending the camels together and
giving glory to God with prayers and supplication and *spiritual
songs*. They performed the *duty* of their service *well* and obeyed
their masters *according to the flesh* in every *command*, fulfilling
the Scriptures, "Obey your masters with all fear, not only the
good and mild, *but* also the perverse. For it is a grace to do so[137]."

19.   IT HAPPENED AFTER SOME TIME, AS HE WAS IN THE FIELD,
tending the camels peacefully and without disturbance, the
wicked devil was unable to bear the sight of such *peace* and entered
the *lawless Berber* whose slave the holy Apa Samuel was. *Then* he
took counsel in his heart, saying, "Why do you leave this servant
without a wife? *But* arise and marry him to this girl[138] who tends

---

136 J. Callender has worked out a paradigm of Coptic locative constructions in
JEA (1973) 190-198: the form used here corresponds to his type (2), in which
time is a relevant factor. The use of the imperf. is quite striking here, for it follows
a series of perfect tenses; I think the sense is 'they began to spend time together
in the field'.

137 cf. I Pet.2, 18.

138 The Coptic word is a *hapax legomenon*; the meaning is clear from the
context. Its pharaonic ancestor may be špnt 'the good quality of a woman' cf. *Aeg.*

your goats, so that he might produce slave children for you who will *serve* in your house." And his heart was pleased with this evil scheme of the *devil*.

It happened when the saint returned from tending the camels in the field, the girl also returned from tending the goats. She was strong in her *body* and evil in her *disposition*, like a *wild beast*, it was said of her that she was able to put a load of wood on her head and carry it to the village, while a strong man could *scarcely* lift it on his back with difficulty. *Then* the holy Apa Samuel came in with the girl, and he said to the saint, "Take this woman here for your wife and assert your *authority* over her. Do with her as you please, and she will be a comfort to you in your exile and you can breed children from her."

The saint was not persuaded by this suggestion, *but* said to his master, "I shall not obey you in this, *for* I am a *monk wearing* a holy *habit*. I cannot *deny* my *habit*, for I have never had sexual *intercourse*." The *Berber* said to him angrily, frowning and shaking his head, "Wicked servant, do you wish to disobey me like the time when you spat in the face of the sun? I can do with you as I please. Do you not know that I am your master? Obey my word. Do not die *miserably* at my hands." The holy Apa Samuel said to him, "I am the servant of *Christ*. I am ready to die for His holy name and to suffer pain in everything you bring upon me, fire, the sword, any death you like, for I shall not pollute my *body*." The *Berber* replied, "So you have prepared yourself to undergo any death? I shall not kill you quickly, *but* I shall tie you to this thorn tree and leave you to die from hunger and thirst until you *acknowledge* to me that you will marry."

So he tied him to the thorn and left him for some days in this *torture*, namely hunger and thirst, the frost of the night and the *burning heat* of the day. O holy Apa Samuel, *citizen* of the kingdom of heaven. Man of heaven, who has sought after the

---

Wb. iv 444. If so, it is perhaps ironical.

things of heaven, the place where *Christ* lives with His Good Father and the Holy *Spirit*.

20.   THEN AFTER THIS THE WICKED *DEVIL*, THE *WORKER* OF *iniquity*, the one who fights ceaselessly with the saints until their final breath, saw that he was unable to overcome him with this snare. He thought of another and assumed the guise of an old *Berber*, a stranger who had come walking in at the time of evening, *so that* he might stay until morning. *Then* the *Berber* whose slave Samuel was, received him until morning. When morning came, the old *Berber* arose and said to Samuel's *Berber* "For what reason is this servant of yours tied to this thorn? See, he is almost dead." The *Berber* replied, "Because he did not obey me (in my wish) to marry him to this young woman. Therefore I have done this to him, with the intention that he should die." The *devil* said, "Do not kill him and lose his *price* which you paid for him[139]. But listen to me and I shall tell you what you might do to him, according as my father did to one of his slaves." The *Berber* said, "Tell me what to do to him." The *devil* replied and said, "It happened in the time of my childhood that my father bought a *monk* for a slave who had been brought from Egypt[140].

He wanted to marry him to a woman, *just* as you do with this one now. *So* he beat him severely and threw them both into the same place and locked the door on them; and in all this he was unable to prevail upon them to have intercourse with each other, except when he brought shackles and placed the hand of the *monk* in them and placed the left hand of the girl in the other side. In this way he bound them and sent them both out to the fields to tend the camels; and so they went with one another. As a result they were with each other by day in the field and slept

---

139   It is difficult to know what sort of price this might have been; information about the sale of slaves at this period is limited cf. Johnson and West *Byzantine Egypt* 132-135.

140   This clever story, which could not fail to capture the Berber's attention, may indicate a regular traffic in monks (and other Egyptians) as slaves.

together at night, until the girl conceived and finally gave birth. In this way the *monk* bred six children for my father, and it is they who *serve* in my house today. *So*, do this yourself, and your mind will be put at rest over him." When the *Berber* heard this from the old man, he was extremely pleased, thinking that it was an old man instructing him. Thereupon he did everything the master of all *evil* told him. *So* the *Berber* put shackles on the saint and the girl.

But lest you hear this and be *scandalised* and think it a weakness of such a perfect one as this, *now* I remind you that I said in the beginning of the proemium, "Be patient and hear attentively." Now I tell you again to be forbearing in *patience*, looking towards the completion of the narrative, so that you may go from strength to strength and *believe* the pains that the saints have suffered for the *love* of God.

It happened that when the *Berber* put the shackles on them both, he said to Apa Samuel, "Go now, and look after the goats with her." Thereupon the girl dragged him this way and that in the goat pen as she *did her work*. *Then* a little later, the goats were sent out and went off to the field. *But while* they were walking along, another *herd* of goats came from the other side of the village. They were on the point of mixing with each other, and the girl rushed over to *prevent* them from doing so. *But* the holy Apa Samuel could not run with her because of the privations of hunger which he had suffered when tied to the thorn, *but* he dragged along behind her. And that *impure* female became very angry and *threatening*, like a mountain boar and a *savage beast*, and she turned to the saint and hit him, saying, "When you see me running after the goats, run with me, lest they stray and our masters *threaten* us." And so she dragged him here and there like a runner[141].

---

141 This sort of violent activity would have been repugnant to monks, who at all times insisted on seemly behaviour: her evil disposition is due to her being an instrument of the devil.

The saint was disturbed, thinking, "What will become of me in this sort of work which is full of shame?" He became very dispirited, saying, "*Truly* it is a great shame to me that I remain *idle*[142], as we live with each other and see each other naked, or that I should see her or that she should see me naked." These were his thoughts as he wept and said, "God, listen to my supplication. Heed my prayer. From the ends of the earth I have cried out to You when my heart has been sad. God, hear me in the sighing of my heart and the distress of my *soul.*" The saint continued to pray and weep sadly.

21.   THEN THE *ANGEL* OF THE LORD APPEARED TO HIM AND said to him, "Why are you weeping and sighing over this trifling affair, and why has your heart become saddened *beyond* all your troubles which you have suffered[143]. *Just* a little longer, and the Lord will make you like a god in the house of Sokortes[144] the *Berber* and all his village. Look, I shall go into the village now and send you one crippled from birth and a mute. *Neither* has the one ever walked *nor* has the other ever talked. *But* stretch forth your hand and cure them. God will ordain His power in you and you will cure them of their diseases."

Then the *angel* went off to the village in the guise of a man. There was a cripple from birth in the village, who was eighteen years old; he had never walked, but *crawled* along the ground, receiving charity. The *angel* of the Lord approached the cripple and said to him, "Have you found *something*[145] today to live on?"

---

142   I think that this is the meaning, though I am not certain whether the word is

143   It is noticeable that the angel, in spite of having been sent to help, will not tolerate the saint's self-pity.

144   This is probably an Egyptian name: Sokri.e. Sobek Gk. Souchos, the crocodile god and -ortes, which means in Late Egyptian 'whom (the god) has given'. I am grateful to Prof. J.Osing for his suggestion about the first part of the name.

145   had acquired the meaning 'payment' by 1st cent.A.D. cf. Liddell and Scott 482. Probably like mod. 'baksheesh'.

The cripple replied, "No, sir." The *angel* said to him, "Arise and go to the east of the village. You will find Samuel, the slave of Sokortes, whose hand is in shackles with that of a girl, and he win *grant*[146] you a blessing, and you will live on it for the rest of your life." When the cripple heard this, he rejoiced greatly. He hurried off, *crawling* along the ground and making his way in haste, until he reached the place where the saint was, with the girl and some others.

When he approached him, he lifted his face up to his. The holy Apa Samuel said to him, "What are looking for?" The cripple clasped his feet and kissed them, saying, "Sir, take pity on me with *something* I may live on today." The saint said to him, "I do not have *anything* with me, my son. But what I have I shall give to you[147]." He stretched forth his hand and took the hand of the cripple, and said to him, "In the name of my Lord Jesus *Christ*, you will arise and stand upon your feet. "And immediately he leapt up and stood upon his feet, and there was nothing wrong with him. He went leaping about, blessing God. He went into the village, saying, "People, come! See this great blessing that has happened to me."

Then the people of the whole village gathered around him, all asking, "What has happened to you?" He said, "Samuel, the slave of Sokortes, he has cured me." And so, the men of the village gathered around the holy Apa Samuel, while the cripple ran before them like a *runner*. And everyone was amazed at what had happened, seeing the saint and the girl with the shackles on their hands. *While* they were gathering around, an old *Berber* woman came up too, with a small child of hers upon her back, about six years old, whose fingers were stuck together and who was deaf and 30 dumb. *Then* this small child came up to the saint,

---

146 This verb is often used of 'cures'.

147 I think there is some conscious literary artistry in this passage: the *double entendre* of , the deliberate use of and the contrast between the phrase 'for the rest of your life' (3) and 'today' (10).

shaking[148] his head and playing with him, *as* was his *manner*, and chewing his clothes. The saint struck him a blow, saying, "It is the Lord Who cures you, *seed* of Canaan[149]". Immediately his ears were opened, and he heard; his mouth was opened, and he spoke; and his fingers were made straight. Thereupon the shackles dissolved like wax on the hands of the saint, and the girl became dumb and *crawled* along the ground in great pain[150], *so that* a great fear descended upon the whole village and the news reached the village *magistrates*.

22.   AND WHEN THE MATTER DID REACH THE CHIEF MAN OF the village, he began saying to his nobles, "If this man has caused the lame to walk and the dumb to speak, this man has the power to work mischief in our whole *country. Now*, let us *make haste* and quickly send him back to his own *country*, and let us not go to Egypt again to bring men of theirs here, *lest* they make us all weak, since their God is *greater than* all the gods'." *Then* the *Berber* whose slave Samuel was, came with his wife and servants, wishing to see what had happened. When they saw what he had done, fear fell upon them all. And the *Berber* Sokortes took the hand of the holy Apa Samuel and led him into his house in great joy.

From that day forward he never again caused him sorrow in any way. *But* he (Samuel) was in the habit of going quietly into the field, as he pleased, tending the camels. And after the girl had been bent double in her head and feet for some days in extreme pain and been dumb, she knew that this great misfortune had befallen her because of the arrogant shamelessness she had displayed towards the holy Apa Samuel. She *crawled alorg* and

---

148 'Shaking' is preceded by , which I have not translated, but which I suspect may be used as an adverb of manner and be not unlike the mod. colloquial 'sort of'.

149 cf. Matt.15, 22.

150 In the manner of the Gadarene swine these infirmities have been inflicted on the unfortunate goat girl.

came to the holy Apa Samuel and clasped his feet and kissed them, weeping, and *begged* him to cure her of her disease. The saint took pity on her and prayed over a little water, which he sprinkled on her. He took her hand and raised her up, saying, "In the name of the Lord Jesus *Christ*, may you stand upon your feet in good health as before." And immediately she arose and stood on her feet, and there was nothing wrong with her.

Thereupon a great fear fell upon the entire household of Sokortes and all his people. They said, "He is a man of heaven who has come down to earth." It happened some time later, *according* to the command of the *Good* God, that the wife of Sokortes became ill: her face, head and whole *body* were in great pain, and day and night she cried out ceaselessly because of the great scourge that was upon her. They would put her on a bed and lay her facing the sun, *so that* the heat of it might relax her whole *body*, but she found no relief. *So,* she spoke to her husband, saying, "Will you not send for Samuel, the man of heaven, to come and heal me from my sickness? Will you leave me to die of this disease?" Her husband replied, "I am afraid of the *laws* of the *Maxyes* and especially our lord the Sun." She said to him, "O that I might be cured! I would give up all my wealth for this[151]!" And so, they sent for the holy Apa Samuel, and he was brought to the village. And the moment the wife of Sokortes saw him, she cried out, saying, "*Welcome*, Samuel, man of heaven. Come and help me in my sickness. Strike me with a blow and cure me as you cured the dumb one and the cripple. Heal my face, head and whole *body*, which is rotting."

The holy Apa Samuel was reluctant to approach her because of the multitude gathered around her; but they kept saying to him, "Approach her, man of God, and heal her from sickness through the *creatures*[152] of your God." The sick woman hastily seized his clothes and drew him to her. She took his hand and put it on her

151   Not an exact translation, but conveys the sense.
152   has, I think, a magical significance cf.Crum 345b.

head, face and whole *body*. The saint said to her, "My Lord Jesus *Christ* will cure you of your sickness." Behold the great miracle beloved, which happened then when the woman leapt up and immediately stood, cured of her sickness. And so, the Scripture was fulfilled in him, "They will lay their hands upon the sick, and they will be cured.[153]

23.   WHEN THE *BERBER* SAW THAT HIS WIFE WAS CURED OF the sickness that was upon her, he prostrated himself before the feet of the *righteous* Apa Samuel, saying, "Your God is the only one, and there is none beside Him." *Then* he begged him to show leniency to him for all the wrongs he had done to him. The woman swore fearful oaths, saying, "I shall never again worship the sun, because it was unable to cure me of my sickness." The woman spoke to her husband, saying, "This man is a god of the Egyptians. *So* let us give praise to him and gifts and send him back to his country, *lest* we upset him and he become angry with us and destroy our entire household."

Thereupon Sokortes sat and spoke with the holy Apa Samuel in words of *entreaty*, saying, "Truly your God is great, because from the first day you came into my house, a great blessing came upon it: my camels have grown numerous and filled my pens, and my slaves have increased and filled my house. So I *entreat* you to perform this great blessing for me and to pray for me and my wife that I should have a small son, for she is barren and has never had a child. I *was patient* with her because she is my sister: my father and her father were brothers, and this great wealth belongs to us both together[154]. Therefore I was unable to throw her out and marry another, a stranger. But I swear to you today the oath of the *Maxyes* that if you pray for me and I have a small

---

153 cf. Mk.16, 18.

154 This may well reflect Egyptian marriage practice, where the woman retained control of her property in a marriage and after it; marriage between first cousins was a convenient way of keeping family property together, and in small semi-nomadic communities family ties were undoubtedly strong.

son, I shall send you back to your country in great honour and glory."

The saint replied to him, "Do you *believe* that I can do this through the power of my God?" The *Berber* said, "Yes, I *believe* that you can do anything you wish through the power of your God." The saint said to him, "My Lord Jesus *Christ*, the Son of the Living God, will reward you *according* to your *faith*." Whereupon God heard the prayer of Apa Samuel. The wife of the *Berber* conceived at that moment. *So* the holy Apa Samuel became a great man in the house of the *Berber* and also in the whole village, so *that* everyone who was sick and in distress, in the moment that they cried out, "God of the holy Apa Samuel may You hear us in our affliction", was immediately restored to health. How many were the healing *graces* that emanated from him in that country, *so that* the sick were brought to him from every place and laid in the place where he *passed by*, and the moment they saw him, their health was restored to them.

Then some days later, the wife of Sokortes gave birth to a small boy, and there was great rejoicing in his whole household. He therefore gave great presents to the saint and thanked him, saying, "Now you shall be free. Anywhere you wish to go, go in *peace*. And again, if you wish to go to your *country* then I shall send you off in *peace* and great honour. If you wish to remain in this *country*, I shall make you my heir. *But* I remind you that I said to you that I would send you back to your land in peace. So, choose for yourself what you wish me to do for you[155]."

24.   THEREAFTER THE HOLY APA SAMUEL SPENT ANOTHER five *weeks* walking in the field with Apa John, not wishing to be separated from him. *But* Apa John *begged* him, saying, "*Since* God has made you free, my beloved brother, do not stay here for my sake. *But* go off to your *monastery*, the place which God

---

155 Sokortes is trying diplomatically to get rid of Samuel, who is now regarded as a potential threat to the community.

has ordained for you[156]. Pray for me in the *monastery* to which you go." Samuel said to him, "Look after yourself, my beloved brother, for everything that has happened to me will happen to you too. You will be chained to a woman like me. *But* beware, do not let desire overcome you, and you will be saved. Later a man of Chalcedon will come here, and you will be sold to him; he will take you to the Pentapolis[157]. *But* take *good* care of yourself, for he will seek after your *faith*, but if you *persevere* in your *faith*, he will release you and send you to your home in *peace*. Now, therefore, I bid you *farewell*, for I shall go back to my *monastery*, the place which the Lord has ordained for me to live in." How great was the multitude of tears of these saints together! Apa John (said), "I bid you *farewell.*" Apa Samuel (said), "You will not see my face in the flesh." Then Apa Samuel said, "Even if we do not see each other again in the *flesh*, we shall, *however*, see each other again in the *spirit.*"

And so they *embraced* each other and parted from one another in great sorrow. *Then* after this, the holy Apa Samuel came to the village that day. The holy Apa Samuel said to Sokortes, "What I should like you to do for me is to send me back to my *country*, because the will of God has come to pass." He was *eager* to perform the wish of the holy Apa Samuel with speed and great joy. *Thus* he gave him a very fine she-camel, which was pregnant, and there was a baby camel walking alongside her. And he gave him great *gifts* which were very fine. He appointed five of his own slaves for him, who were mounted on camels and who knew the desert roads *well*, that they might accompany him and bring him to the boundaries of Amouniake[158] and tell him the road to Kalamun. They returned to their master in *peace*,

---

156 The Greek word for 'monastery' here is

157 It is possible that 'a man of Chalcedon' is miswriting for 'a man of Carthage':

158 The Oasis of Siwa. I am not sure what 'the boundaries' means here; perhaps it means the Bahriyah Oasis, which seems the most likely route to Siwa from the south of the Fayyum cf. Fakhry *Siwa* 15 for the various possible routes.

after having spent seventeen days travelling with him. The holy Apa Samuel went along the road which the *Berbers* had set him on, singing *psalms* and saying, "You have made straight my ways in Your presence"[159], until he reached Kalamun.

25. AND WHEN HE WENT INTO THE SMALL *CHURCH*, HE spread out his hands and gave thanks to God, saying, "I give thanks to You, Lord God *Almighty*, because You have considered me worthy to come to this place again. *For* behold, I shall not die, *but* I shall live until I speak of the miracles and wonders of the Lord, for His mercy endures forever. With teaching has the Lord taught me, and He has not given me over to death[160]." And while the holy Apa Samuel was *still* praying, he experienced *ecstasy* and saw a vision[161]: he saw the holy *Virgin* Mary standing on the east side of the little *church*, with a golden reed in her right hand and with *worthy*[162] men standing on either side of her, giving glory to her; and she walked, measuring with the reed, accompanied by the men. *So* she measured out the northern, western, eastern and southern side. Then he saw a great *throne*, which was very splendid and lofty; it had been set down in that place which she had marked out.

The holy *Virgin* Mary then hastened to sit down on the throne and said, "This is my dwelling-place, where I shall live forever, because I have loved it. And from this time forward I shall establish for myself a dwelling-place in this mountain and I shall dwell in it with Samuel, the servant of my Son[163]. As for these *blessings*, which I had in the *city* of David, Bethlehem, I shall

---

159 cf. Ps. 1, 6 and Is. 40, 3.

160 cf. Ps.117, 17-18.

161 It is perhaps to be expected that Samuel saw his 'patron' in the vision; it is interesting to compare the marking out of the church with the marking out of a pharaonic temple cf.Reymond *Origins* p .210.

162 The Gk. perhaps indicates high rank.

163 Compare this with "Apocalypse*" ed.Ziadeh *ROC* 20,400 "j'y demeure ici avec mon serviteur Samuel..."

cause them to happen in this place, since I have decided to dwell here with Samuel because of his purity, and I shall remain with him forever[164]." Thereupon the *archons* who were following her asked, "Our Lady, will any *Berber* come to this place again?" She replied, "This will not happen, *but* my Son will protect Samuel and his children because of the sufferings he has undergone.[165]" After saying this, she arose and stood up, and Samuel ceased to see her. He *recovered* from the *vision* and rejoiced with a great rejoicing and was glad with the Holy *Spirit*, saying, "Glorious things have been spoken about You, *city* of our God, that You are the dwelling-place of all those who *rejoice* in You[166]."

26.   IT HAPPENED AFTER THIS THAT HE AROSE AND WENT TO the mountain of Takinash and brought his *disciples* to the place which the Lord had prepared for him[167]. Whereupon they *put in order*[168] the *church* and the small *cells*[169]. They *cleared* the area around the *springs* and sowed a quantity of corn and other varieties of seeds around the *springs*. God blessed them and *increased* them, and they became rich in their *fruits, so that* they found their small *needs* from them; and they spent two whole years living on their small *fruits, so that* they never went to Egypt for anything. *So* the fame of their sweet odour went out through all the districts which were about them, *so that* people said to each other, "Great *anchorites* and other saints have settled in this mountain of Kalamun in the province of the Fayyum, *so that*

---

164 A curious reference to her status as Mother of God.

165 In fact Kalamun was attacked in 672 cf. Crum in *Griffith Studies* 210.

166 cf. Ps. 87, 3.

167 Transfer among monasteries appears to have been fairly easy. Unlike western monasticism there are no 'orders' of Coptic monks, though the term 'Pachomian' is sometimes used as if it were an order. This relatively free movement may not always have been conducive to proper discipline e.g. in 1959 Cyril VI ordered all monks to return to their original monasteries.

168 The word here is ; Liddell and Scott 1396b cite a 6th cent, use of the word in connection with a church.

169 These cells date presumably to the previous community.

God will *render* the *Berbers weak* because of the *faith* of these saints and they will not come to Egypt and despoil it again. And the path to Kalamun has opened up to everyone without fear."

So when the fame of the holy Apa Samuel had gone through the whole province, the brothers who lived on the mountain of Neklone heard that the holy Apa Samuel was living in the mountain of Kalamun; fourteen of the holy *monks* arose and came to him and *begged* him to receive them. He received them to him, rejoicing greatly, into a *community as* children. They remained under his *direction*, because they too were God-loving men, who were seeking salvation of their *souls*. *Then* he made a small saline[170] for the brothers to work, and the little camel with her young helped them in everything. Then five more brothers from the mountain of Takinash arose and came to the saint. He received them into a single *community*.

27.   AFTER THIS IT CAME ABOUT THAT APA GREGORY, THE Bishop of the *city* of Kois[171], with Apa Jacob, his *disciple*, heard of the fame of the saint, together with those of his *city*. He went up and came to the mountain of Kalamun, because he had a great pain, which caused him suffering day and night, for he was cruel to the *image* of God[172] and merciless to the poor, gathering insatiably to himself vast amounts of *money*. He spent all night in agony from the pain and did not allow anyone near him to sleep. Then when he met the holy Apa Samuel and spoke with him, he saw the *grace* of God which was upon his face, and at the moment when he embraced the saint, the pain stopped in him,

---

170   Salt was common in the area cf. Azadian, Hug et Munier "Notes sur le Ouady Mouellah" *Bull.Soc.Royale GSog.Egypte* 58 for a description. The monks probably derived a decent income from the sale of salt, though it appears to have been a government monopoly and may have been subject to high tax cf. Johnson and West Byz.Eg.38.

171   Kois was near Oxyrhynchus cf.Amelineau *Geog.* 395. Bishop Gregory appears also in the "Apocalypse" ed.Ziadeh *ROC* 20, 385.

172   cf.Gen.1, 26. A common term for mankind.

and he felt the cure which had worked within him. And so the Bishop was filled with great *faith* towards the holy Apa Samuel.

He spent four days in the *monastery*, and they talked with each other of the greatnesses of God. When he had finished, he went off to his *city* and sent a hundred *solidi[173]* for the *church* and twenty *measures* of oil, together with thirty artabas of wheat and a hundred *jars* of wine. He gave them to the *monastery*, together with a camel and an ass, and said, "*According* as we have heard, so we have seen[174]." *And so* through the prayers of our father, Apa Samuel, the *monastery* was growing daily from one day to the next. It *increased* in the fear of the Lord and *spiritual love*.

28.   SOON[175] ALL WHO SAW HIM WERE LOOKING AT THE *practices* of the man of God, Apa Samuel, and his good examples. After this the holy Apa Samuel girded another seventeen *monks* at once, when they had become *perfect* and *charitable* towards everyone. The brother Apollo was one of the seventeen he had girded, truly the man of God. He would arise in the middle of the night and draw water for the *ministration[176]* and he would sweep the dwellings of the brothers. It was he also who worked on the little camels; when he came from the Fayyum, he was sent to the province[177], and he discharged all the works. *In a word* it was he who loaded up all the handiwork of the brothers and took it to Egypt and sold it, *serving* them with all *zeal* and every *need*. This man Apollo was very solicitous for the brothers. And the holy Apa Samuel rejoiced over him and sang his praises

---

173   It is difficult to know if this is a real or ideal sum, though Gregory was evidently a rich man.

174   cf. Ps.48, 8.

175   The Coptic form of this word is and this probably is a variant of , for the is used to mean 'quickly' only in Classical Greek cf. Liddell and Scott 1762a.

176   The word used here is : Cauwenbergh *Etude* 115 n.l suggests that it may refer to "magasin... cuisine... atelier". Kahle *Bal* vol. I, 39 supports this and supplies references.

177   I understand this to mean that Apollo travelled constantly from Kalamun to the Fayyum.

often to the brothers and frequently paid this tribute which I was fitting to him, "I have found David the son of Jesse[178] who agrees with my heart, this one who does all my wishes. I too have found Apollo, who agrees with my heart, this one who shall give satisfaction to me in all my works."

29.   THE HOLY APA SAMUEL WOULD SPEAK WITH THE brothers in the word of God day and night, speaking and inciting their hearts in the fear of God and His *commandments*, *especially* the "new plants"[179], who had just put on the *habit* of *monasticism*, instructing them about evil and *demonic* thoughts, and he would say, "Do not *neglect* your salvation for a single hour so that it is without *fruit*, for we do not know when we shall be visited. And do not be *neglectful* like the five foolish virgins[180], in whose *life* there was no *good*. *Now*, they went in vain. And so it is with the *monk*, whose *life* contains no *good*, that is, one who is not laden with prayer and *fasting*, that you find him also rich in *passions* and corrupt *desires*, the things which are deadly to the *soul* and the *body* alike. Do not spend one day bearing *fruit* to God and spend another bearing *fruit* to the *devil* in his defiled wishes. Will you continue in works of this nature, or will you spend all your time worshipping vanities? *For* He has said, 'You cannot serve God and Mammon[181].'

Therefore I *beg* you, my beloved sons, do not *neglect* your salvation for a single hour, but keep all God's *commandments* and put upon yourselves the *helmet of faith*[182], and take the double-edged sword of the Holy *Spirit* in your hands and pursue the poison-spitting enemies, that is, the *demons*. And acquire for

---

178   cf. Ps.89, 20.
179   The Coptic form of "neophytes" cf. Ps.144, 12.
180   cf. Matt.25, 1.
181   cf. Matt.6, 24.
182   cf. Eph.6, 16-17. The same text is used in the Rite of Monastic Initiation cf. Evetts in *ROC* ll,60ff.

yourselves a *spiritual vision* of God this Invisible One[183]. And continue to be steadfast in the *love* of His name, which is holy and blessed forever. My beloved children, fight in purity and *peace*, because our fathers, the *prophets*, walked in purity and *love* therefore the Holy Spirit dwelt in them, speaking through their mouths. Therefore the Lord said, "The *Law* and the *Prophets* depend upon these two commandments.[184]"

Behold, you have known that God is in purity. So, work upon your *spiritual* garden[185], which means your *body*, in all purity, so that *Christ* may come to you and make for Himself a dwelling place within you, knowing that the Lord does not dwell in a polluted house, nor does the sinner stand in a place of purity. Have you ever heard that a lion dwelt in the den of a fox, or that a fox dwelt or was able to approach the place where the lion lives[186]? How, my *listeners*, who have promised their *bodies* to God, how can you *tolerate* the wicked foxes, that is, the passions[187] which attack the *authority*[188] day and night, burning up your threshing floors full of fruit, while small flies flying around give an evil smell to your ointment[189].

So, from today forward keep yourselves from committing sin or defiling the holy *habit* which you have received, *lest* God be angry with you and bring down upon you your first and last sins

183   The dem.adj. seems odd here. Is it perhaps def. art.?

184   Cf. Matt.23, 40.

185   A durable image, reaching from John Moschus' *Pratum Spirituale* to Voltaire's advice 'il faut cultiver notre jardin'.

186   A quotation of Shenute ? cf. Leipoldt *Opera* III 79.

187   cf. n.234 (text).

188   This is not really an adequate translation; the term seems to have been taken over from Stoic philosophy, where it describes the authoritative part of the soul. For a full range of its meanings in patristic Greek see the entry in Lampe *Pat.Gk. Lex*. It is possible that its use here, together with the phrase "spiritual vision of God this Invisible One" (1.16), may indicate that Samuel was acquainted with Greek theology.

189   cf. Eccl.10, 1.

redoubled, and lest you incur great disgrace and contempt before all the saints and the Scriptures be fulfilled in you, 'It is better for those who have not known the way of *righteousness* than for those who have known it and returned to their former pollution, like a dog which returns to its vomit and is hated, and like a sow rolling in the mud[190],' and lest you hear this fearful *sentence*[191], 'Companion, why have you come to the bridal chamber with no wedding clothes upon you? How is it that you have come to this place full of pollution and defilement to be cast into the outer darkness, the place where there shall be weeping and gnashing of teeth?'

Therefore I *beg* you, wisely remember that you will leave the *world*, behind you, *or* why have you taken upon you the *monastic habit*? *But* what you came for, seek it *earnestly*. Do you not know, brothers, that your reward before God is great in return for the strenuousness of the *toil* that you have undertaken? Look at the brother monks who have gone before you and who have remained in the *monastic* life for a long time, and imitate their love of God and their good examples. *In a word*, perfect all *holiness* and kindness. Do not be arrogant and boastful, or stiff-necked towards each other, lest the Scriptures be fulfilled in you, 'God opposes arrogance, but gives grace to the humble[192].' Humble yourselves with prayer and *fasting*[193] for it is they which beget all *virtues*. Prayer and *fasting* are the *ambassadors* before God. Through prayer and *fasting* Daniel closed the mouth of the lions, and they could not touch him[194]. Our Lord Jesus commands 'Prayer and *fasting* are the redemption of the *soul*[195].'"

---

190 A fairly free version of II Pet.2, 21ff. quoting Prov.26, 11.

191 cf. Matt.22, 13.

192 cf. Jas.4, 6.

193 cf. Ps.35, 13.

194 cf. Dan.6, 22.

195 cf. note 96 (p. 35)

30.   BUT NOW LET US RETURN TO THE REMEMBRANCE OF OUR
holy father Apa Samuel, giving praise to God on the day of his
holy commemoration, and we shall *make* you *joyful* about the
time when he began to build the great *church*, and how the
faithful people came to them, for his children grew and *increased*
in the fear of God, as they gathered about him daily, the Lord
blessing them and alighting upon them and their children, we
are blessed in the Lord Who created heaven and earth[196]. When
the holy Apa Samuel had prepared everything for the building of
the *church*, Apa Joseph the *Bishop* of the Fayyum[197] assisting him
in all things, they *began* to build, the Lord helping them with
everything they *needed*.

And Apollo was in Egypt with some brother *monks* and a number
of camels were sent to them for their *use*, for all the *governors*
of Egypt heard that the holy Apa Samuel had *begun* to build a
church in the valley of Kalamun. Therefore Apollo was often sent
for and brought to the *cities* and villages; and every *necessity* for
the building of the *church* was given to him, while they *requested*
in great *faith* the blessing and the prayers of our holy father, Apa
Samuel, that it (i.e. the blessing) should be in their homes and in
their fields and upon their animals; they had great *faith* in him.
All men who lived in Egypt said, "Because of the prayers of the
holy Apa Samuel and the sufferings he has undergone, God has
restrained the *Berbers* and not let them enter Egypt to this day."
So he was to the neighbouring districts like an *apostle* of God;
they sent him great *gifts* and *presents* for the *building*.

---

196 Doxological.
197 The Fayyum had clearly reverted to Monophysite 'orthodoxy*. It is not
known whether Joseph succeeded Victor directly.

31.   THE MENA, THE *EPARCH* OF THE CITY OF PELHIP[198], A
relative (?)[199] of the holy Apa Samuel, heard that he had started
building a *church*. He was very pleased, *so* he *appointed* his son
to govern the *city* in his absence and loaded ships with great
provisions, whether it was wood *or* pitch *or* iron, *in a word,*
every *need* that they might *require,* and he sent them down to
the *monastery.* And our fathers have borne witness that he also
brought fifteen hundred *solidi* and gave them to the *monastery,*
together with *whole silk* cloth for the adornment of the holy
altar[200]. And thus he did not leave him until the *church* was
completed in all splendour, they having *decorated* it *beautifully.*
The brothers started to *consecrate* it in the name of the holy Apa
Samuel. *But then* when he heard of this, he leapt up and said.
"God forbid! *Rather* it is in the name of the Lady of us all, the
holy *God-Bearer* Mary that it shall be *consecrated,* together with
the small *church* and all the *chapels* in Her name. *Believe* me, my
children, that after four *generations* God will raise up a *leader* in
this *monastery:* it is he who will build the *church* in my name[201]."

When the brothers heard these words from the man of God,
they were silent and gave glory to God for the things that were
to happen in due course. *So* after they had completed the *church,*
they sent for Joseph, the *Bishop* of the Fayyum, to come and
consecrate the *church.* He came in great joy, accompanied by great
magistrates of the *city* of the Fayyum. When the *Bishop* entered
the church, he was very pleased and said, "*Truly* this is the place

---

198   It may be doubted whether Mena was really the Eparch. Pelhip, equated
with Masil cf.Amelineau *Géog.* 244ff., was in the Eparchy of Egypt; the latest
Byzantine compilation places the diocese of Milleos (Metelis?) in Eparchy A of
Egypt cf. Ball *Eg. in the Class. Geographers* 176. However, he was obviously in
charge of the city and was able to appoint his son to administer it in his absence.
199   The Coptic reads 'noble'but I think makes better sense.
200   The altar covering was usually of silk cf.Butler *Anc.Copt.Churches* II 208.
201   If this is to be taken literally, then it means the latter half of the 8th cent.
The monastery must have been flourishing indeed, for a church to Misael was
built c.end of 8th cent. cf. *Patrologia Orientalis* III 443ff.

of forgiveness of sins. This is the place where God lives with His *angels*. This is the house which the Most High has purified. God is in its midst. It shall not be moved. *Truly*, as we have heard, so we have seen in the *city* of the Lord of Hosts[202]."

The *magistrates* also gave their *gifts* to the *church*, *according* to the Scripture, "The *magistrates* of the *people* brought their *gifts* to the *church*.[203]" And the *Bishop* held a *catholic* service. Thereupon he *consecrated* the *church* in the name of the Father and of the Son and of the Holy *Spirit* and of the Holy *God-Bearer*, the *Holy* Mary. And straightaway he caused the holy Apa Samuel to be brought to him against his will and *ordained* him *presbyter*, together with Apollo, Apa Djidjoi and Apa Selbane; he also ordained Apa Theodore the Canopite, Zachaeus and Shenute and made them *deacons*, *beside* another six whom Apa Samuel caused Apa John[204] to ordain; testimony has been borne of Theodore the Canopite that he often spoke with the *Virgin* Mary face to face owing to the purity of his *body*, and furthermore Zachaeus did the same as a result of his good conduct. And he completed the consecration of the *church* in great joy; each went back to his place in peace.[205]

32.   NOW WE HAVE BEEN TOLD BY OUR FATHERS ABOUT A *widow* woman living in the *city* of Pemdje[206] with two young *virgin* daughters of hers: it was said of her that she set aside three *measures* of oil a year and sent them to the *monastery* so that she and her children might be remembered. It happened on one occasion that she sent them *as usual*[207] and Apa Apollo, the *minister* brother, undertook to put them inside the cell; when

---

202 cf. Ps.48, 8.

203 Might this be an allusion to Acts 4, 34-35?

204 For Joseph.

205 According to the ritual given in Horner *Consecration* vii a bishop requires seven presbyters for the consecration of a church; presumably Samuel, Djidjoi, Selbane, Theodore, Zachaeus, Apollo, and Shenute assisted the bishop.

206 Oxyrhynchus.

207 At least part of the income of monasteries took the form of regular donations.

he came to put down the vessel, he stumbled over another that was full, and both were broken. Apollo, the *minister* brother, was grievously upset and hastily came out and threw himself at the feet of our holy father Apa Samuel, saying to him, "Forgive me, my holy father, for I have sinned." But the old man said to him, "The Lord Who sent them is the One Who has required them. Go and collect what you can."

Apollo took two brothers with him to go and collect the oil. And when they entered the cell, they found the Vessels floating upon the oil; whereupon they gathered oil until other empty *vessels* were filled, which they had found by the blessing ordained for them by the Lord through the prayers of our father Apa Samuel. But if there are some who *disbelieve* this miracle, let them listen to me, and I shall *convince* you from the *Scriptures* concerning Elisha the *prophet*, *for* our father Apa Samuel is also a prophet.

As to Elisha the prophet, a woman[208] came to him, saying, "My *Lord*, help me, for my husband has died and the *creditor* has taken off my two children and made them his slaves." Elisha said to her, "Ask what you want me to do for you; tell me what is in your house." She said, "I have nothing, not even in my house, except a little oil which I anoint myself and my children with. Elisha said to her, "Go and *ask* a neighbour for some empty *Vessels* and do not hesitate to ask for many *vessels*. Go into your house and close the door on yourself and your children, and pour oil into your *vessels* from that which is in your jars[209] until you fill them."

She closed the door on herself and her children and poured oil into the *Vessels* until they filled up to the brim. She came to the *prophet* and told him what happened. He said to her, "Go now

---

208 cf.II Kings 4, 1-7.

209 There is some confusion here between the ownership of jars: it should properly read 'pour into these vessels (which you have borrowed) from the oil which is in your jars', though in the text of the Septuagint the widow has only one jar of oil.

and sell the oil, and redeem the *lives* of your children; *as for* the rest of the oil, you can live on it with your children." Now you know that the One Who *worked* through Elisha is the One Who worked through the *righteous* Apa Samuel, because at all times God is glorified through His saints.

33.   IT HAPPENED AFTER THIS THAT THE HOLY APA SAMUEL sent brothers to gather reeds. *So* he set up a little *hut* in the place where they were working[210]. *Now* there were two brothers in the *monastery*, who were born at the same time; and they were God-loving men, who obeyed our father: the name of one was Hatre and the name of the other was Houmise[211]. So our father sent my brother Hatre to cut reeds. Some days later he lay down and was ill. The brothers bore it with fortitude, saying, "*Surely* today *or* tomorrow he will get up." Therefore they did not send him back.

Later the illness became more serious, and the pains of death came upon him. *So* the brothers took a beast and mounted him on it, with the intention of taking him back to the *monastery*; he was unable to sit on the animal because of the *distress* caused by the illness which was upon him. Thereupon they put him down and laid him in a *hut*. They sent a brother to the *monastery* to announce to our father, "Our brother Hatre is ill and near to dying." When the old man heard this about the brother, he called Houmise the brother of Hatre and two other brothers; he sent them to Egypt[212], saying to them, "Go and say to the brother Hatre, 'Your father Samuel says that you are to rise and come quickly, because he wants to see you; he does not wish you

---

210   It was a common practice in Egypt for those working at some distance from home to set up a hut where they could stay overnight without having to return home; remnants of the huts built by the workers in the Valley of the Kings, for instance, have been discovered cf. Bierbrier *Tomb Builders* 53.

211   Hatre means 'twin' and Houmise means 'birthday'.

212   The word for Egypt is very like the word for 'reed'; it is possible that they went due east, perhaps as far as the Bahr Yussuf, but there were probably enough reeds around Kalamun to make this unnecessary.

to die outside the *monastery*.'" The brothers departed from the old man.

Hatre himself died in the night when the brothers came to him. The holy Apa Samuel was making great prayers and supplications night and day for him before God. As he continued to do so, behold the Holy *Virgin* Mary came to him with a joyous face. She said to him in great joy, "Why is your heart sad and why are you weeping? Look, Hatre, the man you sent for, has died. Have courage and be strong. I shall raise him from the dead and make him come to you here, and you will see him, together with all the brothers. Afterwards he will sleep. Because you have given glory to me, I shall give glory to you." When the Holy *Virgin* had said this to him, she ascended to heaven in glory.

34. THE HOLY APA SAMUEL CONTINUED TO PRAY AND *GIVE thanks* to God and wait for what would happen[213]. When morning came, the brothers washed Hatre and closed the *hut*, waiting for the news that would come to them. As they were *still* sitting there, behold, Houmise came, accompanied by the brothers. He prostrated himself upon his face for a long time, weeping bitterly and saying, "Woe to me, my brother! My father sent me to you so that you should come to him. But I now find that you are already dead." And when he said this, weeping bitterly, Hatre opened his eyes and said, "Is it my father Apa 15 Samuel who calls me?" He answered, "Yes, it is he who calls you." Immediately he leapt up like one who had never been ill. He made his way to the road where the brothers were waiting, and they asked him. "What has happened to you?" He said, "I am afraid to reveal these things, *lest* God become angry with me." The brothers said to him, "No, our beloved brother, God

---

213 This translation supposes a syntactical emendation of the Coptic, which has 'when he continued...', but is not followed by a main clause; I have made 'he continued' a main verb.

would not be angry with you, it is written in the *Scripture*, 'It is good to reveal the works of God for the glory of God[214].

Furthermore it says in the Gospel, 'What you heard with your ears, proclaim it on the roof-tops[215].' "Apa Hatre said, "I was taken to the underworld[216]. I saw it, a spacious dwelling place, encircled in great glory. There was *neither* sun *nor* moon in that place, *neither* night *nor* day, *but* it was the Light of God Which illuminated them (sic). Then I was taken to a dwelling place, planted entirely with a tree which was laden with fruit[217], and there was a great glory surrounding them; and many saints lived there; and these offered delicious *fruits* to my mouth, rejoicing greatly with me. They said to me, 'This is the home of Apa Samuel and all his children who will follow him and his good example.'" His brother Houmise said, "My brother, what happened before you were allowed to come to us?[218]" Hatre replied, " When I came from that place, all the saints rejoicing with me, behold, a Man of Light called as many as three times, 'Hatre, Hatre, come, behold, your father calls you.' I followed him rejoicing greatly. And when he brought me to the *outer* door, I saw you."

As they talked of these things, they approached the *monastery*. The holy Apa Samuel gathered together the brothers of the monastery, knowing that Hatre had come. When the brothers saw Apa Hatre, they embraced him. Our father, Apa Samuel, said to him, "*Welcome*, my God-loving son, whom God has loved and received to Him." When Hatre saw him, he hastened to *prostrate*

---

214 cf.Tobit 12, 11.

215 cf. Matt.10, 27.

216 I read this phrase as the Coptic prep.and def.art. 'to the' followed by the , used in the same sense as , though this seems to be attested only in Aeschylus cf.Liddell and Scott 335b. For the association of visions with death cf. Kosack *Legende* 50.

217 The tree of life perhaps?

218 Houmise is eager to establish the exact sequence of events and emphasises the clause 'before you were allowed...' by using an emphatic 'second' tense in 'what happened'.

himself and embrace him, and then he lay down and gave up the *spirit*. Our father threw himself upon his neck, weeping and saying, "Blessed are you, my son, the *celestial* dwelling-places have been opened to you. Blessed are you, for you have seen that which the *angels desire* to see. Blessed are you, my son, for you have become a holy gift of God[219]." He then caused his body to be prepared for burial and placed in the middle of the *church*[220]. They spent the whole night meditating[221] around him. On the following day he raised up the offering[222] for him; they *celebrated mass* and took him out and buried him, giving glory to God for the miracle which had happened.

35.   AFTER THIS EVERYONE BEGAN TO COME TO HIM FROM everywhere, coming to the holy Apa Samuel to receive blessing from him and teaching about the salvation of their *souls*. He taught each one of them about what was good for their *souls*. But he was grieved, for they did not allow him to be at peace, and they began to trouble him a lot. *So* the Holy Spirit instructed him about what was good for his soul and the whole *monastery*. He *thus* brought to the fore Apa Apollo and *appointed* him over all the brothers in his stead; and he gave him *authority* to do anything, like himself. Our father retired to great seclusion, like Elijah on Mount Carmel[223]. There was a small marsh on the west side of the mountain called *Piliheu*[224], about half a day's journey from the *monastery* at Kalamun. Our father, Apa Samuel, took with him the holy relics[225] and he went down there and did not come up to the *monastery except* once every three months.

---

219   cf. I Pet.1, 12 and Rom.6, 23.

220   Presumably the church of the B.V.M.

221   also means 'reciting (prayers)'.

222   i.e. the Eucharist.

223   cf. I Kings 18, 42.

224   Not attested elsewhere as a place name, though it occurs as a personal name e.g. the Bishop of Helwan cf.Müller *Kana* 35

225   These were presumably contained in a box and represented the remains of holy men who had died at Kalamun; Samuel took them either for spiritual

36.   THEN ON ONE OCCASION AN *ORDER* WAS ISSUED[226]: THE
camels of the *monastery* and those of everyone else were
requisitioned to take corn to Klysma. Those of the *monastery*
were taken, as I have said, and for six whole months were not
released. And so they were unable to find a way of transporting
bread for the brothers[227]. *So* because of the great multitude who
came to them and the alms which they donated to everyone,
whether great *or* small, in consequence, they almost ran out of
bread, and Apa Apollo called to the *steward*[228], "Go and take
care of the brothers and those who will come to us today," for it
was the day of the Holy *God-Bearer*, the *Holy* Mary[229], when the
multitude came to them.

The *steward* said to him, "We shall not find bread for the
multitude; there is *hardly* enough for the brothers today." Apa
Apollo said to him, "Go, and what you will find, set it before
them, and God will bless it." The *steward* went and did so. He set
it before the multitude, and the Lord blessed it. They all ate and
were satisfied. Apa Apollo was *distressed* because he was not able
to find our father Apa Samuel that he might bring the matter
before him, that the bread had run out: he was in the western
mountain because of the great multitudes who were troubling

---

comfort or perhaps for safekeeping.

226 This may refer to an event recorded in Baladhuri *Futuh at Buldan* (tr.Hitti)
216: in A.H.21 i.e. 643/4 the Caliph 'Omar ordered ?Amr to send corn from
Egypt to Medina because there was a shortage of it. The most obvious point
of departure for Medina is Suez (Klysma). It is difficult to be certain of the
chronology, but by this time Samuel would have been at Kalamun for about five
or six years.

227 They had clearly stopped being self-sufficient, as they were for two years at
the beginning; indicates an increase in the population of the monastery.

228 The steward was responsible for the supplies.

229 This might refer toi the Birth 1 Bashons (26 April) or 10 Thoth (7 Sep.), the
Death 21 Tubeh (16 Jan.) or, perhaps more likely, the Assumption 16 Mesore (9
Aug.), the day when Samuel set out from Takinash for Kalamun.

him[230]. When evening came, Apa Apollo said to the *steward* "Take care of the brothers for now and tomorrow. God willing, we shall send them to Egypt that they may load small quantities of bread on their backs and bring them to us." The *steward* said to him, "My father, with what shall I take care of them? There has been no bread since yesterday, and there is nothing in the store except for just a few scraps and a few crumbs." Apa Apollo said to him, "Go and sweep the store and prepare a little food for the brothers, with a few dates, that they might eat it now. *Only* do your best to take care of them, and I *trust* to God and the prayers of my holy father Apa Samuel that God will give us our appointed portion for tomorrow also."

The *steward* did *as* Apa Apollo had said to him, and he went to the store-room door, with the intention of opening it. Apa Apollo stood and spread out his hands and prayed, saying, "God and the prayers of my father Apa Samuel, will you hear me today when I cry out to you, and will you also send your blessing upon this store of bread belonging to the holy *monastery* for the sake of all the multitudes who come to us from everywhere." Apa Apollo was *still* saying this prayer, when the *steward* arrived to open the store-room door, but was unable to do so; he looked in through the hole in the door and found the store full to the door, even to the roof. When he saw this great miracle which had happened, the *steward* rejoiced greatly; he went off to tell Apa Apollo what had happened. The holy Apa Apollo thanked God and the prayers of the holy Apa Samuel. The brothers accompanied Apa Apollo and went and found the store full to its door. *So* they took off the roof[231] and brought forth a great quantity of corn, until they

---

230 According to the paradigm laid out by Callender in *JEA* 1973 p.197 the locative construction used here is of the 'generic-durative' type, where time is irrelevant; it is more than likely that time had become irrelevant for Samuel in his seclusion.

231 I am not entirely certain of the translation, but the removal of the roof from an Egyptian granary would have been relatively simple. As far as I know only one is known from an archaeological site cf. Walters *Monastic Arch.* 103.

were able to open the door. Everyone who heard was amazed and gave glory to God Who alone performs these miracles[232].

37.   WHEN OUR FATHER APA SAMUEL CAME OUT OF THE desert, they told and he rejoiced greatly. He spent some days in the *monastery* with the brothers, instructing them all in the fear of the Lord. And the holy Apa Samuel returned as before to the *marsh*. *Then* when he had returned to his place, he put off coming to the *monastery* to visit the brothers for six months, for the Forty Holy Days overtook him at that time, and he was in a great and rigorous period of *asceticism*. *Thus*, as a result of the extreme *asceticism* which he practised, he succumbed to a great physical illness, like all the saints[233]. He continued to lie there and was unable to get up, *celebrating mass* alone; *nor* did he find any man who would *minister* to him. *Thus* all the *demons* of the mountain gathered and came to the door of the small *church*[234] where he was lying ill. They cried out in a fearful voice, "Let us go in and bring him out, for His God has abandoned him. Let us now take our revenge on him, for this time he has come into our hands[235]."

Thereupon they came into him with swords and staffs and lances in their hands, striking terror like *Berbers*, saying, Let us slay him and kill him": others said, "Let us not kill him, but let us leave him, for he will die in due course alone[236]."' The saint was silent, thinking, "My God, *help* me, for I have lifted up my *soul* to You, my God. Let me not be ashamed, *nor* let my enemies rejoice over

---

232   The writer would no doubt have the Feeding of the Five Thousand cf. John c.6 in mind.

233   Excessive fasting was probably a major cause of illness among monks and was often discouraged cf. 113,7ff.

234   Samuel had evidently built a small chapel for himself.

235   The modern Egyptian has a great fear of the evil spirits of the desert, the 'afarit'. Here they are credited with the human desire for revenge, for the saint has dared to trespass on their territory.

236   cf. earlier 89, 40ff.

me[237]." As he was thinking these things, sighing, the Lord sent His angel to him. When the *demons* saw him, they vanished like *smoke*. The angel of the Lord took his hand and raised him up, and said to him, "Do not be afraid; the Lord is with you. Why are you afraid?" And he offered *spiritual food* to his lips. When he received it, great strength came to him; he arose and made an act of worship before God and His *angel*; and the *angel* took away the fear from him and went up to heaven.

Our father Apa Samuel rejoiced over the grace of God which came upon him, and he came up from the *marsh*, wishing to visit the brothers. As he was walking along, the *devil* assumed the guise of a cripple and stood before him. The old man said to him, "Where on earth have you come from?[238]" The *devil* said to him, "Who taught you these things? Whose example do you follow?" The saint replied, "I follow the example of the great *ascete* Antony.[239]" The saint said to him, "What do you want with me?" The *devil* said, "*So* you follow the example of that one? He and those like him have *ruined* all those in my power. He has *hurt* them a lot." With these words the *devil* changed into a *leopard*, fire issuing from his mouth and nostrils, and advanced upon the old man in an *illusion*[240], terrifying him greatly. The old man stretched forth his hands and prayed, "Lord, incline your ears and hear me, for I am a poor man. I am a wretched man. Have pity on me, Lord, for I cry out to You all day." As the holy old man was *still* praying, the *devil* became as smoke and vanished. The old man continued his journey to the *monastery*, *meditating*.

---

237 cf. Ps.25, 2 and Ps.35, 19.
238 The Coptic has lit. 'from where in this place'.
239 The Coptic uses an emphatic tense: 'it is the example of the...that I follow.' cf. earlier 87, 36.
240 The word used here is , which can mean both 'illusion' and 'pomp, display'; perhaps both are intended here.

38.   It was said of Apa Stephen the *presbyter* and *disciple* of Apa Samuel that he was a great ascete. It was testified of him that he spent a long time, as many as eighteen years eating no food *except* herbs of the field. *Thus* as a result of his extreme and prolonged *ascetic practices*, he became very ill. He ordered[241] a little food to be prepared for him that he might eat and recover his strength. *But* he refused, saying, "I shall not eat anything cooked *under* any circumstances until the Lord visits me[242]." Our father said, "*Believe* me, Stephen, you will eat cooked food and drink wine, and you will eat more than these things, which are not *fitting* to the *monastic life.*[243]" When Apa Stephen heard this, he wept bitterly and was *grieved.*

Samuel said to him, "Why do *grieve* about this small thing which you have heard from me?" He replied, "I *grieve*, my father, for perhaps you have seen ruin coming upon me?" The saint said to him, "Do not *grieve*, my son, for I was not talking to you about ruin coming upon you; *but* you *will* become a bishop[244] and you will receive your *enjoyment* of all *good* things." *Thus* it was not long before the *prophecy* of Apa Samuel was fulfilled: the brother became ill and was taken to a *monastery* in the mountain of Pemdje that he might drink the water of Egypt in that place[245]. Then after Apa Stephen had spent a few days in that place, the fame of the saint filled all places *both* in the *city* *and* in the villages, because of the cures which he made of the sick. After some days, the *Bishop* of Pemdje died; *so* they took the

---

241   The subject is presumably Samuel.

242   i.e. until he dies.

243   The Coptic word for 'eat' here means 'swallow, submit to', as if it were something unpleasant (it is interesting to note that English has the same idiom); perhaps a further indication of 'anti-clericalism'?

244   Stephen may have been the first of the 'orthodox bishops who came out of the holy monastery (Kalamun)' cf. Homily on Samuel ed. Simon *Miscellanea Biblica* 1934,171.

245   The water around Kalamun was undoubtedly salty and hardly fit for one suffering from malnutrition.

holy Apa Stephen and *consecrated* him *bishop*, that he might tend the flock of God in fear and *sobriety;* he continued to give praise to God and Apa Samuel.

39.   THERE WAS *ALSO* TALK OF A GREAT *ASCETE* IN THE *MONASTERY* who performed great and many *feats of asceticism* day and night. It was testified of him that he spent twenty years in *conduct* of this nature, without *desiring* a day of human society[246]. *Thus* finally the *devil* brought upon him great gluttony in an overwhelming *desire*. He continued *therefore* in great suffering of this nature[247]. He said to himself "What shall I do in the midst of the brothers? I shall not be able to eat, *nor* shall I be able to drink *and particularly* since this great name 'ascete' is applied to me. *But* I know what I shall do. I shall arise and take myself away from this place and go to another *monastery* somewhere else where they do not know me, and I shall take my *needs* in it; and nobody will know me." He called to his two *disciples* and said to them, "Pack your clothes together[248] and prepare yourselves, so that at midnight we may arise and go."

Now the holy Apa Samuel knew in *spirit*. He arose hastily and called Apa Apollo and told him everything which had happened to the *ascetic* brother. He sent him to the door (of the brother's cell), saying, "Sit down here. If he tries to leave, seize him. Do not let him go, for he is a good old man with his sons. You will instruct him and his sons in the Holy *Scriptures, according* as I have shown you[249]." Apa Apollo the brother came to the door of

---

246   Clearly a great monastic virtue, which conferred strength on those who practised it. Julius Caesar observed this strength in the Belgae 'fortissimi Belgae, propterea quod a cultu atque humanitate provinciae longissime absunt' cf. *De Bello Gallico* c.1.

247   The Coptic for 'continued' is actually a sort of periphrastic 'he continued remaining', which perhaps aims to emphasise the state.

248   I am not certain of the meaning of this phrase: an alternative rendering might be 'get dressed'.

249   This phrase seems to mean that Samuel has instructed Apollo to use certain Biblical passages to convince the old man.

the brother, lay down and covered his face. When the old *ascete* prepared himself to leave, he said to one of the *disciples*, "Arise. Go and see if the Place is *quiet* before we leave." When he came out, he found Apollo lying on the floor, his face covered. He did not know him *nor* did he speak to him. *So* he turned back to his father, saying, "There is a man sleeping at the door." The old man became angry with the brother. He said, "*To be* sure you do not wish to come with me, if you seize upon an excuse like this." He *prostrated himself*, saying, "Forgive me, my holy father, I am ready to come with you to any place you will go. *Only* go and see for yourself."

The old man came and saw Apollo sleeping. He did not know him, *but* he thought it was a *layman*. He walked up to him, lifted up his cloak and revealed his face. Apa Apollo said to him, "Where are you going, my beloved brother? Why have you not found one of the brothers to reveal your thoughts to him, so that you now follow your heart's wish and waste all your effort for comfort of this *world*? Paul says, 'Drink a little wine[250].' He also says, 'The troubles of this *world* are not worthy of the glory that shall be revealed to us[251].' And further, 'What a man sows, this shall he also reap[252].' And, 'He who sows in tears shall reap in joy[253]. 'Have you not read them or *meditated upon* them? *Rather* have you allowed the *desire* for food to overcome you?" When the old *ascete* heard these things from Apa Apollo, he *prostrated himself* before him, saying, "Forgive me. I have sinned in my lack of reflection. I *beg* you, my father, to instruct me concerning this word which Paul wrote to Timothy, 'Do not drink water, *but* drink a little wine for the sake of your *stomach* and your many illnesses.'"

---

250 cf. I Tim.5, 23.
251 cf. Rom.8, 18.
252 cf. Gal.6, 7.
253 cf. Ps.126, 5.

Apa Apollo said, "I shall teach you the interpretation of this saying, according to what the Lord puts in my mouth, *for* you are not unaware that Paul often wrote to Timothy, saying , '*Fight the good fight*[254] and 'Stand up Quickly as a chosen one of God, a *worker* who is not ashamed'[255]. Timothy fought in just this way, so that he spent many days without eating and without drinking, through his love of God. *And so* his anus itched within him; when he took a little food, he would cast it forth from his mouth because of the extreme pain. Also when he drank water and urinated, Timothy was in great pain and cried out in excruciating agony. For this reason Paul wrote to him, 'Do not drink water, *but* drink a little wine for the sake of your stomach and your many illnesses,' for wine is blood in the *body* of man: it seeks not to flow away like water, but is blood which remains in the *body* of man." In this way the *ascete* was encouraged by the words of Apa Apollo and he returned to his former *asceticism*, until he ended his life well in joy, giving glory to God and the holy Apa Samuel[256].

40.   OUR HOLY FATHER APA SAMUEL INCREASED IN HIS DAYS like Moses, the *archprophet. Now,* the *prophet* Moses lived one hundred and twenty years[257]. Our father Apa Samuel lived ninety eight years: he spent eighteen years before becoming a *monk*[258]; after this he spent sixteen in the mountain of Scetis; he spent another three and a half years in the mountain of Neklone

---

254   cf. I Tim.6, 12.

255   cf. II Tim.2, 15.

256   It is noticeable that Samuel does not wish to forbid the monk's asceticism, but merely wishes to encourage him to exercise self-control, and does so with masterly psychology.

257   The 'theme' of this chapter is the comparison between Samuel and Moses; woven into it is Deut.34, 7. Elsewhere in the text Samuel has been compared to Abraham, but Isaac has judged it more prudent to choose Moses for comparison here: Abraham was a hundred and seventy five when he died and had several concubines.

258   There has been some confusion here: Samuel decided to become a monk at eighteen, but did not leave home for Scetis until he was twenty-two cf. 7, 2.

and six months in Takinash; he spent three years in the *captivity* of the *Berbers*, and he spent another fifty-seven in the mountain of Kalamun, which is his *monastery*.

He had great divine power in him; he never *needed* anyone else to help him like all the other old men. *Neither* did his light *dim nor* did his *reason* or *mind* change[259]. *But* his word was strong, and he made prayers and *fastings* with great *zeal*, not allowing anyone to precede him to *church*.

41.   IT HAPPENED ONCE AS HE WAS STANDING AT PRAYER THAT an *angel* of the Lord stood over him and said to him, "*Hail* Apa Samuel the *anchorite*. *Hail, archimandrite* and great *ascete*. *Hail, judge* and father of the *monks*. *Hail*, Samuel, who has fulfilled all the *commandments* of the Gospel. *Hail*, the one who has often been a *martyr* without shedding blood[260]. *Hail*, the one who has built the *tent* of Abraham and received God and His *angels*. Blessed are you, Samuel, for you have laid down your *life* for your brothers, *according* to the *commandment* of the Gospel,[261] 'There is no greater *love* than this, that a man should lay down his *life* for his friends.'

Now the Lord is with you. It will be *yet* another eight days before He seeks after you to give you the *inheritance* of Abraham, Isaac and Jacob[262]. Have courage, Samuel. Your death is not death *but* life everlasting. Since you have given glory to the Lord and His *Virgin* Mother, He will give glory to you and send the saints to meet you, these whose example you have imitated, namely, Basil, Gregory, Severus, Antony, Macarius, Pachomius and Apa

---

259   cf. Deut. 34, 7.

260   This passage would seem to confirm Samuel's status as a martyr, the ideal for the Copts: it is no accident, I think, that the Christian era in Egypt begins with the Year of Martyrs i.e. 284, the accession year of Diocletian, who instigated the greatest persecution of Christians c.303.

261   cf. John 15, 13.

262   A similar phrase occurs later cf.119, 9, which might perhaps be emended to 'inheritance of the saints'.

Shenute the *archimandrite*, these whom you have imitated.[263]" When the *angel* of the Lord had said this to him, he went up to heaven in glory.

42.   IT HAPPENED WHEN OUR FATHER APA SAMUEL FELL ILL, there was a great fever upon him, and he was giving thanks to God, looking forward to the hour when the Lord would visit him. *So* when the brothers saw that he lay down and was ill, they all gathered around him and continued to comfort him; and they kept *begging* him to utter a word of comfort to them. When the old man saw that the illness had become heavy upon him and that the brothers *asked* him to utter a word of God to them, before he went to the Lord, he *then* sat in their midst and spent the whole night talking to them in the word of God and giving courage to them, saying, "You are the sons of promise, even as Isaac was the son of promise[264]. *For* you, My children, are my pride and my crown in the Lord[265]. Moreover, continue in that in which you are, namely, the *love* of your fellows. *Thus* be enduring in all the *commandments* of the Holy *Gospel*, each one edifying his neighbour in divine faith[266]. Do not *slander* one another *or lie* about one another, but love one another with a holy love, bound to prayer and *fasting* in holy *faith*. You know, my beloved children, that I have often made mention to you of prayer and *fasting*, that it is they which make man new again and a companion of God and His *angels*.

It is said in the *wisdom* of the *Greeks* that he who wishes to be separated from God, let him *violate* prayer and *fasting*. If the *Greeks*, who do not know God, *commend* prayer and *fasting* as

---

263   Basil of Caesarea (329-379), Gregory Nazianus (329-389) or Gregory of Nyssa (335-395), Severus of Antioch (465-538), Macarius the Egyptian (c.300-390), Pachomius (292-349) and Shenute, the celebrated Abbott of the White Monastery at Sohag in Upper Egypt (333-451).

264   cf. Gal.4, 28.

265   cf. I Thess.2, 20.

266   cf. I Thess.5, 11.

the great *principles*, then *how much more* should we, the children of the Most High God[267]. *So*, pray in all things, whether you eat or drink. And do all things for the glory of God. When you sit down to eat with each other, let nobody look into the face of another to see how he eats, *but* let each one look to himself alone. And further, as you walk along the road, pray that the Lord will send His angel to guide you.

Moses prayed and defeated Amalek, so that the sons of Israel found the way and went to the Promised Land[268]. Elijah also prayed and raised up the son of the *widow*[269]. Again he prayed and brought fire out of heaven[270]. Peter prayed, and the Lord sent His angel and saved him from prison[271]. Elisha prayed seven times and raised up the son of the Shunamite woman[272]. Peter prayed and raised up Tabitha, who was dead[273]. Susanna prayed in her heart as she was about to be taken outside to be destroyed, and God saved her from death and shame[274]. Moreover prayer and *fasting* saved the Three *Holy* Ones from the furnace of Nebuchadnezzar[275]. Nothing is possible *except* through prayer and *fasting*. Believe me, my children, there are more than sixty

---

267   I am not sure quite what the phrase 'wisdom of the Greeks' means. Works of pagan philosophers were not unknown to the Copts; a selection of their works in Coptic may be found in Till *Kopt. Gramm.* 267. Coincidentally Till quotes an interesting parallel to the first part of the sentence (ibid. §466) 'the heathens who do not know God'. I have not, however, been able to consult this text. It is possible that the term 'principles' (kephalaion) may be an allusion to the works of Evagrius Ponticus "Kephalaia Gnostica": Evagrius was both philosopher and ascetic, but his speculative thinking made him suspect (not unlike Origen), and the term 'Hellene', used frequently of pagans in Coptic texts, may be a veiled insult on a dubious Christian.

268   cf. Ex.17, 8.
269   cf. I Kings 17, 7.
270   cf. II Kings 2, 11.
271   cf. Acts 12, 9.
272   cf. II Kings 4, 18.
273   cf. Acts 9, 36.
274   cf. Bk Susanna
275   cf. Dan.3, 19.

brothers among you who keep all the *commandments* of the Lord; and they have fulfilled them with fortitude and have overcome the Adversary[276]. So, my children, keep all the holy commandments which have been ordained to you by your fathers."

43. WHEN THE HOLY APA SAMUEL HAD FINISHED UTTERING these words to the brothers, he turned his face upon Apa Apollo and said to him, "Behold, I shall go to the Lord like all my fathers. Therefore, I commit the brothers to the Lord and I commit them to you, that you may take care of them *according* as you do now. Do not *scandalise* any of them, lest he destroy his *soul* and God require his blood from you; and *not only* you, but everyone who shall follow you, if they cause the brothers to stumble and spoil their *services* and *meditations*, I shall require their blood from them before God and His *angels*, and they will become strangers to me and all the saints."

When he had said these words, he ordered all the brothers to *celebrate the mass*, for it was the middle of the night[277]. They subsequently spent a further six days assembled about him daily, both day and night, as he lay in their midst with the illness lying very heavy upon him. In his great love for them, he ordered each of them to *recite* his *off-by-hearts*[278], while he listened to them, rejoicing: they numbered a hundred and twenty *monks* surrounding him[279]. When they reached the night of the seventh day of Khoiak (and) the morning of the eighth day, on the night

---

276 One of the names of the devil. Note that he addresses 'more than 60' monks, whereas later in the text the total complement is given as 120. Does this mean that there were certain grades of monks?

277 Most likely a combination of the night office and Mass cf. Evelyn-White *History* 208.

278 The English is an exact translation of the Greek. Lefort has discussed the term in *Mus.* 34,175; he concludes that it can also mean 'a haute voix'. The two meanings are possible.

279 cf. n.264.

of which he was to die[280], at the time of evening, when the sun was about to set[281], his *mind* was taken up to heaven, and he spoke his *heavenly* words, a great fever being upon him.

The brothers surrounded him, all of them weeping and saying, "Woe to us, our father is going and leaving us orphans." Whereupon the holy old man opened his eyes and saw them weeping. He said to them, "Why are you weeping?" They replied, "We are weeping because you will go and leave us." He said to them, "My children, do not weep. It is to the Lord that I am going." They said to him, "Why, father, have you spent this long time staring and not spoken to us?" He said to them, "I saw my Lady, the Holy *Virgin* Mary, with a great multitude following her, *wearing* white robes. My heart turned after them and I continued to stare after them, *so that* my mind was taken up to heaven." When he had said these words, great joy appeared on his face. He smiled and a great perfume was diffused. At that moment the holy Apa Samuel opened his mouth and gave up his *spirit* in peace. Amen.

The brothers continued to weep, saying, "*Truly* God has deprived us of a *righteous* father. We have become *orphans*." The brothers took him, washed him and brought him into the *church*. They placed him in the middle and *begged* Apa Apollo that they (should be allowed to) *greet* him before he was prepared for burial. He did not *distress* them, *but* said to them, "Come forward, each of you, and *greet* him each *according* to his *rank*." *Thus* they came forward one by one and *greeted* him, Apollo himself holding the hand of Apa Samuel and placing it upon the head of each of the brothers.[282]

44.   O THIS GREAT MIRACLE THAT HAPPENED AT THAT TIME, it is not something that can be passed over, *but* it behoves us to

---

280   The morning hour was 6 a.m.
281   Perhaps a conscious 'literary' touch about this?
282   Does this mean that Apollo was to succeed?

proclaim it *according* as our fathers have testified to us. *For* they have said that there was a *cantor* in the *monastery*, a man of the *city* of Pemdje, whose name was Christopher. Our father put him in the *monastery* because he was blind from birth[283]. He had spent fourteen years *singing* in the *church* with the brothers; God had *granted* him knowledge and *wisdom*, and he had learned the entire *psalmody* of the *church*. Our father loved him as a *perfect monk*. He too came to receive the blessing of our father, being guided on his way; *for* he had attained to his little tunic, which was upon him[284], weeping bitterly and in distress, because of the good things which the old man had done for him. *Thus*, when they had led him to the *body* of the saint that he might *greet* his *body* and take his hand to put it on his head and face, at the moment when his hand touched his eyes, they opened like those of everyone.

How great are the *graces* which came forth from the holy Apa Samuel. *Truly*, our *righteous* father has found great *influence* before God, that He should forgive our sins.[285] And they wrapped up his *body* and caused the *archdeacon* to sit in the middle of the *church* and he recited the *Lamentations* of Jeremiah the *Prophet*. Afterwards they *celebrated a catholic mass* over his revered *body*. They took him out, buried him and spent seven days in mourning for him, spending many nights of vigil, with *psalms* and *spiritual songs, celebrating mass* over him[286]. He went to rest on the eighth day of Khoiak, having completed a ripe old

---

283 The occupation of musician is a traditional one for blind people in many societies e.g. Homer was said to be blind.

284 I am not sure whether this means that Christopher had actually reached the tunic of Samuel or (more likely, in my view) that he had recently been granted the right to wear the monastic tunic. If the latter, it may be that he had just been initiated as a monk.

285 'Influence' renders the Greek , a quality given to those who have led a blameless life and denied those who have sinned cf. Budge Coptic Martyrdoms 285. Literally it means 'freedom of speech', but by extension I understand this to mean the ability to intercede with God.

286 Presumably Mass was said each day of the mourning.

age pleasing to God. He received (his) *inheritance* with the saints (or, perhaps, of the saints).

45.   I ENTREAT AND *BEG* YOU, MY HOLY FATHER APA SAMUEL, to entreat God on my behalf that He should forgive all the faults which I have made in the *narration* of your *angelic life*. *But* I have uttered these few things *according to* my ability, *to* the extent of the poverty of my weak *mind*. *Thus* we *beg* you, our father, to remember us before *Christ* the Son of God, Who redeemed us with His own blood, that we may find mercy and *influence* in His presence, and forgiveness of our sins and *transgressions* on the Last Great Day. May it happen to us all that we obtain mercy in His presence, we Christian[287] children. Through the *grace* and philanthropy of Our Lord Jesus *Christ*, through Whom there is all glory fitting to Him and His *Good* Father and the Holy *Spirit*, Which is Creator and Consubstantial[288] now and at all times.

---

287   This seems a peculiar phrase; perhaps it serves to distinguish themselves from the growing population of Muslims.

288   The 'classic' term of Nicaean orthodoxy.

The Apocalypse of Samuel of Kalamun

An English version by
Anthony Alcock

THE ARABIC SOURCE TEXT OF THIS TRANSLATION IS THE ONE
published in *Revue de l'Orient Chrétien* vol. 20: 376-392 by J.
Ziadeh. The numbers in the translation are those of Ziadeh's
publication. Ziadeh himself divides his text and the translation
that follows it (pp. 392-404) according to the page numbers of
the Arabic manuscript. I have consulted his translation, but my
version is based on the Arabic text. I should make it clear that
I am not an 'Arabist', that is to say, I have no formal training in
that language. I have incorporated the Arabic text from Ziadeh's
publication, so that each page of Arabic comes directly before
the English version.

The document is a sermon that looks into the future. The Arabic
word in the title means something like 'treatise, discourse'. The
manuscript, Paris no. 150, containing the text is dated to 1322
AM (=1606 AD). Samuel's prophecy about the Arabs is briefly
mentioned in the Synaxary (Patrologia Orientalis III, 408). F.
Nau, in his note following Ziadeh's publication (p.406), believes
this text to be a translation of an 8th cent. Coptic original

'dont on retrouvera peut-être quelques fragments au Faioum'. Optimism should never be discouraged.

There are several versions of the life of Samuel, the most important being a complete text in Sahidic Copticin the Pierpont Morgan library, one of a large collection of early medieval books from the monastery of St Michael at Hamouli (abbreviated in the notes to VitaSam).[289] There is also at least one Arabic version, which is in Franciscan Centre of Christian Oriental Studies in Cairo. It is an extremely late version that was produced on Sept. 29 1945.[290] There are probably others which I do not know about.

I have mostly used the future tense that uses the auxiliary verb 'will', in keeping with the

English language conventions of prophecy. Samuel experienced the Arab conquest of Egypt, but apart from one unspecific reference in VitaSam,[291] there is no mention of this event or the presence of the invaders in the country, and it is fairly clear from this reference that the writer of it did not know or even care very much where the order for the requisition came from.

Language is an important factor in the text. In the early days of the Arab Conquest, Egyptians were no longer obliged to use Greek, the language of administration of the time, and were able to produce legal documents in their own language[292], but inevitably Arabic replaced Greek as the official language. By the time this text was composed there was obviously a feeling that Christianity and the practice of it were under attack from Arabic, and it is probably why Athanasius of Qûs wrote a grammar of Coptic in

---

289 *Life of Samuel of Kalamun by Isaac the Presbyter*, ed. and tr. A. Alcock (1983). References to this are made according to the paragraph numbers arbitrarily assigned by the translator to the text.

290 *Le Muséon* vol. 109 (1996): 321-345 and vol. 111 (1998): 377-404.

291 [3] §36: camels requisitioned to transport grain to Suez.

292 For example, the substantial quantities of 8th cent. legal texts from Jême, the town which had grown up around the mortuary temple of Ramesses III on the west bank of Thebes.

the 13th cent., in Arabic of course[293] Since Christianity, unlike Islam, has never regarded any one language as the sole language in which God spoke to Christians, it is difficult to imagine that there would have been any 'faith-based' reason for resenting the use of Arabic in Christianity, but it is not difficult to imagine that the Christian population, as it became increasingly smaller, was beginning to resent the conversions to another religion that many people must have been able to witness on a daily basis. The travesty of Islam that is presented on p.378 of the text is undoubtedly due to an excited fit of rhetoric.

---

293 With the relatively bizarre title of *Qilâdat al-tahrîr fi'il 'ilm al tafsîr* (Necklace of writing in the discipline of interpretation) ed. and tr. Gertrud Bauer (1972).

A Discourse of Samuel, Abbot of the Monastery of Kalamun

In the name of the Father, the Son and the Holy Spirit, the One God. To him is glory. Amen.

We begin with the help of the Lord, praise to Him, to write the discourse of our holy father Anba Samuel, abbot of the monastery of Kalamun, may his prayer be with us. Amen.

In it he spoke of matters relating to the things which will happen in the land of Egypt in the kingdom of the Arab hegira.[294] The discourse was attended by Gregory Bishop of Kais,[295] who had come to visit him and be cured of his illness, I mean the bishop. Apollo[296], the disciple of the holy Anba Samuel, expects [297] this spiritual counsel to benefit those who read it, memorize it and do what is written in it.

When the kingdom of the Arab hegira was over the land of Egypt, there were few of them. They multiplied their blessings on the Christian people. At that time monastic brothers spoke with the father Anba Samuel about them and asked him if their kingdom in Egypt would last a long time or not, the saint sighed deeply from the depths of his heart in the presence of the bishop and said,

---

294   I have kept this term throughout. It probably refers here only to the 'immigration' of Arab Muslims into Egypt. E.W. Lane *Arabic-English Lexicon* (1863) p. 2880 says that the primary meaning of the term indicates removal from desert to town and ultimately emigration from one's own country.

295   The episode is described in some detail in VitaSam §27. Gregory is obviously in some pain and is accordingly fairly unpleasant to people around him. He is also apparently greedy. But he is eventually cured of both his illness and covetousness by Samuel. There is no indication of prophecy. Indeed, the only 'prophecy' mentioned in VitaSam is in §38 concerning Stephanos the Presbyter, who is to become Bishop of Pemdje (Oxyrhynchus)

296   For his key role in the practical affairs of the monastery cf. VitaSam cf. §§ 28 ff

297   An intriguing verb, and one can only speculate about why the writer of the text uses it.

"Blessed be God, Who has established times and limited them, Who lowers one nation and raises the other and changes kings and sets up other kings. Do not, my beloved sons, think that this nation is favoured with God because He has delivered the land into their hands. No, the wisdom of God is inscrutable to man, and there is no-one who knows the works of the Creator or the end of times except One alone. I will instruct you, my children, in the many evils committed by heretics on the orthodox in the time of our father Dioscorus and, even today, and also the many evils that were done to our father Dioscorus, the fact that they exiled him to remote islands. His see was occupied by Irotarius while he was still alive. And this Irotarius[298] committed many injustices on the Christians. He banished bishops and killed the orthodox, ruined the monasteries. And as for Uqilianus[299] of the false schêma (monastic habit), I will say nothing of him. I am unable to speak and describe the wickedness of the things done by him in the city of Jerusalem and his killing of the orthodox, which was also done by the wicked figure whose name is unworthy to be mentioned, Kabirus the Muqauqiz,[300] wicked in his deeds, the one who oppressed the orthodox greatly and drove them from place to place. He himself was at great pains to seek out father Benjamin, grinding his teeth about him and

298 Dioscorus was exiled to the Island of Gangra after his failure at the Council of Chalcedon. His Constantinople-appointed successor, Proterius, was lynched by the Alexandrians after a couple of years.

299 The name Uqilianus is a copyist's error, probably for Ufilianus: the bearer of it seems to have been a monk. If it refers to Juvenal the Patriarch of Jerusalem, the Egyptian hostility to him is probably driven by Juvenal's support for the condemnation of Dioscorus at the Council of Chaledon.

300 Kabirus is Cyrus, sent by Sergius Patriarch of Constantinople to Egypt in 631 to try to reconcile the Egyptians to Constantinople by means of a modified formula known as the Monothelite doctrine, which was considered to be possibly acceptable to Monophysites. His nickname refers to his origins in Colchis on the Black Sea. He negotiated the so-called Treaty of Misr with the invading Arab army. His reputation among the Copts seems to have fairly negative, Francois Nau produced a short note in Le Muséon 45 (1932): 1-17 suggesting that he might have had the reputation of being 'un trafiquant de chair blanche'

saying, "May I find him of the long beard so that I can order him
to be stoned."[301] This is why God heard the prayer of the elect
who implored him and sent them a nation who were seeking
gold, not a religious creed,[302] according to their request.

I choose silence, my beloved children, and I do not wish to
explain to you what will happen to the Christians at the hands
of the nation of the Arab hegira in their days. May you not utter
any mention of them among us today, for they are an intractable
nation. They should not be mentioned in assemblies of the
saints. Oh! This name, which is the hegira and their kingdom
and is counter to our laws, these high and mighty kings who
have their day. Many are the tribulations that will happen to the
coming generations because their deeds will truly follow them,
my children. Angels of the Lord have told me of the difficult
times and the many tribulations that will happen to the sons
of man through this arrogant nation. I do not wish to converse
about these Arabs and their kingdom and the end of times, as is
written, 'It is not for you to know the time and times, because
the Father has put this under his sole control[303] ', but I will tell
you about what is conducive to the benefit of your souls, and this
is what I say to you, 'It is inevitable that there will be in coming
generations a time when you abandon the commandments of
God, but everyone who has an alert heart will take care not
to imitate the deeds of the hegira and his soul will be saved.
My children, have you seen this nation of small size? It will
inevitably grow and they will become a very great people and
different nations will blend in with them and increase like the
sands of the seashore and locusts. Their kingdom will dominate
and they will occupy many towns to the east and west and they
will occupy Jerusalem many times and many nations will blend

301 Benjamin is described in VitaSam §7,20 as 'he of the long beard'.
302 There is probably a wordplay here in the Arabic that cannot be reproduced
in English: dahab (gold) and madhab (religious creed)
303 Acts 1,7

in with them, the Garaganin, the Abranin, the Yunanin and Raha'in who are from Amid, the Amamin, the Kaldanin, the Fars, the Berber, Sind and Hind[1]. They will raise their kings and stay for some little time in peace with the Christians. After that, the Christians will envy them in their activities, they will then eat and drink with them and they will play like them. They will behave like them and fornicate like them. They will take a harem like them and defile their bodies with women of the hegira, who are transgressors and defiled. Like them, they will have intercourse with men. They will steal, swear and commit injustice like them. They will hate each other. They will deliver each other to merciless nations. Many vain words will come forth from their mouths, which it is not necessary to say. They, human beings, will make an image of God in many ways. Some will call them pigs, dogs and donkeys. Similarly, Christian women will also abandon the decorous habits that of orderly women and will become blasphemers, vain with loose garments, extremely shameless in their conduct. They will also utter words of blasphemy. Words will come forth from their mouths which it is not necessary for anyone to repeat. They will blaspheme against God until they dare to say without fear, "I will have an effect on God[2] who created me."

Woe and again woe! What can I say about deeds of this sort, which anger God the Perfect One? If God were not merciful and patient in spirit, He would not give the world respite in truth. Christians will adopt evil practices in that time and they will

---

1 Georgians (perhaps), Hebrews, Greeks, Raha'in (perhaps related to the word 'arha" in Lane's Arabic Lexicon p.133 meaning 'independent tribe, in no need of others') from Amid (perhaps related to the word for 'extremity'), Amamin (perhaps related to the adjective meaning 'anterior' as in 'nuqta amamiya' meaning an 'outpost'). The rest are easily identifiable. Sind was conquered by Muhammad bin Qasim in the 8th cent. and the so-called Delhi Sultanate was set up in the 12th cent

2 This sounds as if it might a colloquialism similar to the BrE: 'They'll do you', meaning 'They'll punish you'

lose interest in the things of God, distracted by the objects of their desire, and in this time they will be desirous of eating and drinking, desirous of pleasures more than the love of God, they will be more attached to places of eating and drinking than to churches of God. They will spend their time sitting in streets and market places, caring about the affairs of the world and without any interest at all in the church and they will pay no heed in their hearts that the chapters are being read and passing them by, so that they no longer hear the Gospel. Indeed, they will attend Church only after the end of the Mass. Some of them will do things which it is not fitting for them to do, because they are consumed by their desires until the chapters pass them by. They will attend Church and take the Gospel and read the chapter that has been read and go into a corner by themselves, read it and make their own law for themselves.

Woe and again woe! My beloved children, what can I say in these times? And about the great idleness that grips the Christians? They are in that time when they move away from uprightness and are like the hegira in their works. They call their children by their (Arab) names and abandon the names of the angels, prophets, apostles and martyrs. They also do other things. If I told you about them, your hearts would be greatly distressed. They are abandoning their beautiful Coptic language often used by our spiritual fathers to pronounce the Holy Spirit. They teach their children from childhood to speak Arabic and they are proud of it. And they do it in the sanctuary.

Woe and again woe! My beloved children. What can I say about these times when the reading is made in the church and no-one understands what is being read or what is being said, because they have forgotten their language. They are truly wretched and deserve our tears because they have forgotten their language and speak the language of the hegira. Woe to every Christian who teaches his son to speak the language of the hegira from childhood and forget the language of his fathers, he is at fault, as it is written, "The fathers will be judged for their sons."[3] What can I say about the dissolution that is happening to Christians, who eat and drink in the sanctuary without fear and forget the fear of the sanctuary, for whom the sanctuary becomes as nothing? The doors of the sanctuary are neglected and there is not even half a deacon to watch over them because they consider the seven sacraments that belong to the Church of little importance and they do not perform them. You will find people in this time who are seeking any grade of priest, because they no longer deserve to be readers who read to the people. Many church books become useless because no-one can understand them any longer. Their attention is diverted to foreign books and they become oblivious in that time of many of the martyrs, because their lives become unnecessary and you will not find any of them at all. The few still existing, even if they are read, many people do not understand what is read because they do not know the language. Many churches in that time will also become empty ruins on feast days and Sundays. No-one is found to read the Book of the Anbal[4], let alone the Forty Holy ones, which are for our salvation. You will not find anyone to read to the people or preach, because they are oblivious of the language and do not understand what they are reading or doing. The reading also is unintelligible to them, even in Arsinoe the great city in the Fayyum and all its districts, where the laws (or, possible nomes) [5]of Christ are. The blessed in their books, the strong in the knowledge of God are those in whose

---

3 I cannot identify this quotation

4 Possibly the pulpit (ambon), the book being the Gospel. The 40 holy ones may refer to the books of the Old Testament.

5 Arabic word is the plural of 'nomos', which can also mean an administrative district. The Fayyum is a distinctive part of the country, fed by an arm of the river that ends in a lake. It was chosen by the Ptolemies (in the early 3rd cent. BC) as a place to settle veteran soldiers, perhaps because there would, initially at least, be little contact with Egyptians. A number of largely Greek speaking cities over the next hundred years was the result. It was probably no more Christian than any other part of Egypt, but there may be echoes of Rufinus' glowing account of the monastic life of Oxyrhynchus (Historia Monachorum in Aegypto Chapter 5).

mouth is the Coptic language, as sweet as honey and as fragrant as perfumes because of the beauty of their pronunciation of Coptic. In this time, they will all abandon it and speak Arabic and glory in it to the point where they no longer know that they are Christian, indeed one will think that they are Berbers.[6] The remainder who continue to live in the South, who know Coptic and speak it - their Christian brothers who speak Arabic will attack and insult them.

Woe and again woe! How great in truth is this sadness and these things that Christians will do in that time. My heart grieves greatly as I describe to you these events and my eyes weep and my body feels greatly. Do you think that there is any other pain for the heart greater than this, to see Christians abandoning their sweet language and glorying in Arabic and in their names? I say to you in truth, my children that those who forsake their holy names and give their children foreign names, which removes them from the blessing of the saints and emboldens them to speak in the sanctuary in a foreign language. Things are quite different now from the days of our fathers, when people do great wrong and there is no-one to correct them or teach them or grieve over them because all their hearts are in error, their elders and teachers. The father learns the faults of his son and the mother approves of her errant daughter and does not correct her, but joins her in sin. Sin is not a weeping matter for them, but is empty for them because they are without teachers. For this reason, sins multiply and there is no-one to teach them to weep for them, but every one of them does what he wants, the priest does not weep for the sinner, the elder does not teach the younger and the younger does not heed the elder, because they have abandoned the canons of the Church and the laws of our holy fathers, so that they will avoid the mandatory and known fasts, and the others who fast do not complete their fasts as is

---

6   This may reflect the Classical Greek meaning of people who do not make intelligible sounds. Berbers, however, were not really too far away from Kalamun.

necessary because of their stomach and persuade other people to break their fast with them because every one of them is a law for himself.[7] as he wishes. There are other people who, for social reasons, break fast before the time that is appointed before the different times of sunset each month. You find them in the church, lounging and idle. They speak with each other about vanities of the world. They do not do not think at all or recall that the body of God is on the plate and his blood in the cup in the sanctuary. Indeed, the awe-inspiring secret with them is like a plaything. And if one of them is with God so that he says a word of teaching of the canons, they consider him an enemy and open their mouths against him, like the lion. Women gossip too much in the church and are neglectful. There is no-one to reply to them. The apostle Paul says, "Women should be silent in church, cover their heads."[8] The priests will become lax and distracted. They will not observe the right teaching, If a priest is interested in saying a word of teaching, he will say it with boredom and without any burning passion for the people. God will become angry with them because they ignore the laws of the church and the teaching of our spiritual fathers. He will put them under the hateful domination of the hegira Arabs, who will cause them to lose much and impose heavy intolerable taxes on them. They will be in great poverty. The hegira will destroy all the things on the land because of the heaviness of their domination. They will impose great losses on the widows and orphans. They will abuse the elders and oppress the young women and detain them in their houses because of taxes. They will insult Christianity. Priest and monks will be humiliated by them. They will eat and drink and play inside the churches. They will have intercourse with women before the altar without fear and they will make the churches of God into stables for their horses and tie up their horses and transport animals there. The powers of the church

---

7 This is the second time that the concept of 'law to oneself' has been used. An echo of Romans 2:14?

8 I Cor. 11,5

will go and rise to heaven when they see with their own eyes the disgusting things done by this people in the churches. They will demolish many churches and raze them to the ground, taking way their timber, bricks and stones. They will use them to build for themselves liwans [9] and large houses and remove the crosses from the churches. Many churches will be transported and made into mosques because of their pride and hatred of Christians. The saints and martyrs will see the deeds being done in their shrines and will complain to God and will say, "O God, who is divine right, judge between us and this nation which is doing these things in our churches. O God who is good, do what is right and give them their due for their deeds." Jesus Christ, the Word of the Father and Only Son will appease their hearts and console them, saying, "Be patient, my beloved and blessed ones, until their time comes. Everything you see of their works is because of the sins my people has committed. They have abandoned my counsel and commandments and are like this nation. For this reason, it will have power over them until its time is completed. The saints and martyrs in the present time will turn from their supplications and will be patient until the time of the hegira is completed. Know, my children, that this nation will do much evil and wickedness in Egypt. Their kingdom will be very strong and their yoke will be heavy like iron. Their people will increase like locusts and they will occupy many towns, which will come under their power. Their tyranny will grow greatly in Egypt until the country is ruined by much oppression. They will eat, drink, play and dress like bridegrooms. They will glory greatly, saying, "No other nation will ever have power over us." They will survey the earth with the measuring rod and they will take taxes. There will be great inflation in the land. Many people will die of hunger and will remain discarded because there is no-one to bury them. People will sleep in their houses at night and when

---

9   In this context it probably means no more than a hall surrounded by a large house.

they awake, they will find on their door three notices demanding a loss or ruin of some sort, from big cities, small villages and ports. Egypt of these large trees and gardens will become salty and scabrous because of the many taxes levied on the country by people who are proud and have little mercy. Their yoke is like iron. They will oppress the people and demand gold. They will count the people, great and small, and record their names in registers. They will demand gold for their persons (poll tax). People will sell their clothes to make up for their losses. They will take everything people possess, giving reasons which, they establish for them and impose on them. People will move from city to city and town to town. They will seek rest and will not find it. While they are in these difficulties, they will continue in the blindness of their hearts. They will not understand the guidance the Lord gives them. They will not repent. They will not ask for instruction of the church. But they will add to the total of their sins because pride will be uppermost in the Christians of these days. They will try to dominate each other. They will annihilate each other. They will mock the Holy Scripture which is of God Himself. Even the priests, the monks and those who serve the holy altar, they too will do this sort of thing. They will boast and say, "I am more steadfast than our fathers." They will forget the Scripture that pride in men is repellent to God. As long as they do this, this nation will have power over them and will punish them as it is written, "If they despise my laws and do not keep my commandments, I will chastise their error with the stick and beat their idleness with the rod."[10]

My beloved children, may what is written in the Psalms not come to pass over us, but let us ask God not to leave His people until the End. Let him turn His anger into mercy and His wrath ito peace and look upon His Christian people in that time and remember His bride the Church. May He send them help from heaven. May He not act with them according to their sins and

10 Ps. 89,31ff.

deal with them according to wrongdoings. I now advise you, my beloved children, and have a humble request of you to advise those who come after you to the completion of generations to keep themselves perfect and not allow Christians to speak Arabic in these places. This is a great judgement, because they are multiplying in this time and dare to speak in the language of the hegira in the sanctuary.

Woe and again woe to those who are like this. I have heard from an elder at worship, wearing the spirit and perfect in holiness. He said to me when I asked him about the matters of the hegira, he said to me, "My son, Samuel, understand what I say to you. In the time when Christians dare to speak in the language of the hegira in the sanctuary, this is when they will blaspheme in it against the Holy Spirit and the Holy Trinity. Woe to Christians in that time! Woe seven times over!

If I begin, my beloved children, to tell you the sayings of that holy elder, my discourse will increase. But let us desist from this. What I have told you is enough. Those who have a heart that understands, let them understand. Those who keep themselves from the things of the hegira, they will not be like them and will be able to save their souls."

When the holy elder Anba Samuel finished his discourse, he turned to Anba Apollo and the assembled brothers and said to us, "Lo! You have heard with your ears some of the tribulations to be experienced by future generations who will dare to change the sacred laws and pure teaching of our fathers. I have made known to you the greatness of the calamity that you will experience too, my beloved children. Take care and wake up, for goodness and blessings are for those who take care and wake up.

Now, my beloved children, take care and wake up, for goodness and blessings are for those who act in accordance with apostolic commandments. Let us exert ourselves at all times, my beloved children that we may remove ourselves from diabolical desires and let us not follow the desires of our hearts and bodies, because the devil leads the heart astray and casts his thoughts and desires into it, so let us flee from our desires. Christ will bless us with good things in His everlasting kingdom.

Advice

TAKE CARE, MY BELOVED CHILDREN, NOT TO BE NEGLIGENT. THIS is the root of all pains and breeds all poisonous plants.

Take care, my beloved children, and flee from lust, for lust makes reason cloudy. It prevents people from waking up to knowledge of God.

Take care, my beloved children, not to be too concerned, for this alienates people from the benefits of paradise.

Take care, my beloved children, not to be defiled, for God and His angels will become angry.

Take care, my beloved children, not to be proud, for that is the chief of all evils and alienates man from God.

Take care, my beloved children, not be vainglorious and dictatorial, for these ruins every effort of man in the sight of God.

Take care, my beloved children, not to be cowardly in the virtues, for the coward who is weak of heart is the one who becomes idle and is full of every sin and every vain thing. If you are cowards and are too weak of heart, you will become negligent in your laws and lazy in your prayers and efforts. You will thus refrain from observing the laws of God. Indeed, be lion-hearted and cast from you every thought that opposes you and remove yourself from every bodily rest, the breeding ground of poisonous plants.

Take care, my beloved children, not to engage in adultery, because adultery sacrifices many and casts them to the ground. Those whom it takes to hell do not return.

Take care, my beloved children, do not befriend a youth or child and do not enter the place where there are women, for when the stone rubs against the flint, fire comes from it and burns much matter.[11]

Take care, my beloved children, and flee from all evil things that cast man into hell and deliver him to punishment. Do the works of goodness that lead to the kingdom of Heaven. These are: purity, humility, prayer, fasting, asceticism, patience, exertion, endurance, charity, peace, sweetness, brotherly love, acceptance of pain, humbleness. Cast away from you all idleness, all destruction, all anger, all weakness of heart because our fathers indeed completed their lives in great humility in hunger and thirst, refraining from drinking any wine. The disturbances caused by lust are in the limbs of man from too much wine-drinking. Wine increases shameless lust. It cuts the flesh of the body and, in general, most wine depresses the Holy Spirit. Our fathers knew much of the sadness that comes from wine from the beginning. They refrained from it. Indeed, a little of it was used in illness. The great ascete Timothy was allowed to drink small quantities of wine for his illness and many sicknesses.[12] What shall I do about those at the height of youth who develop strong pains. My beloved children, all observance of the commandments is good. Humility is a great benefit. What humbles the soul saves it. It conveys it to the port of salvation and is full of the good things of heavenly Jerusalem. Now, I advise you strongly to continue to restrain yourselves and do what I advise you and observe the laws which have been handed over to you. Advise your children to tell those who come after them until the end of generations to come that they observe and keep to the monastic works that they may deserve the legacy of the heavenly kingdom. For there

---

11 Arabic form of the Greek

12 A fairly well-known passage (1 Tim. 5, 23), also used in VitaSam, to justify giving wine to a monk whose stomach may have suffered from the ravages of excessive ascetic practices.

will be[13] a time when many monks will relax and play and there will be blasphemy about the monastic life because of them. They will discard the laws and obligations[14]... the land of Egypt the great ones by the right of those who wear the Holy Spirit and by the right of the great Antony, Apa Macarius, Apa Pachomius, Apa Shenoute[15], those by whose intercessions Egypt continues to exist and those who have imposed the laws on us and imposed them on monasticism. As for us, we have done their upright deeds and we have listened to their holy teaching and kept to it. As for you, my beloved children, heed what I have said to you today and every monastic declaration which our spiritual fathers have set for you, advise those who come after you in generations to come to heed every word that I have said to you today, as the Apostle Paul, "Be like me, as I am like the Messiah."[16] So, my beloved children, be like me and follow in my footsteps, as I have followed in the footsteps of my holy fathers. If you heed what I have advised, the Mother of God will ask her beloved son for you, because you are in her dwelling place, as I have seen with my own eyes many times. I have seen her with my eyes in this church and heard her with my ears, saying, "This is my dwelling and I live in it, because I love it, with my servant Samuel and his children who will come after him and seize his advice."[17] You must, my beloved children, complete well all the advice and

---

13 The prefix indicating the future is used here.

14 There is clearly a problem in the text. Ziadeh's translation ignores the next few words, which may be rendered tentatively as 'the fixed star of the past luminaries of the land of Egypt', but the passage seems to be corrupt and best left to an Arabist for repair.

15 Miss spelt as 'Shaloudha'. The error is probably a writing error: the dot over the 4th letter belongs to the 2nd letter.

16 I Cor. 11,1

17 VitaSam § 25, in which Mary measures out the ground for a new church after Samuel has returned to Kalamun after his captivity in the Siwa Oasis. Measuring out the area for a new temple was not uncommon in pharaonic Egypt, e.g. detailed account of the foundation ceremony at Edfu on the N.E. wall of the Outer Hypostyle Hall.

monastic rules. If you complete them, you will deserve to see the Mother of God, the Blessed Virgin, Our Lady Mary, as I myself have seen here. She has promised many blessings for those who will occupy this desert and who visit it, seek blessing in it, ask forgiveness for their sins.

Blessed are you, my beloved children, because you deserve to live in the dwelling place of the Pure Virgin, Our Lay Mary. You sing and bless God in this church chosen by the Virgin as her dwelling place.

Blessed is the one who comes to this church in faith. I say to you, my beloved children, that the Mother of God, Our Lady Mary, will ask her beloved Son to be kind enough to forgive our sins. Blessed is the one who offers sacrifice in this holy church. I say to you that the Mother of God will intercede on his behalf with God that He receive his sacrifice in heavenly Jerusalem. He who makes a vow to this church and hastens to fulfill it, I say to you that she will accept his vow and fulfill his request with all speed. He who writes this holy discourse and puts it in the church to be read for the benefit of the souls of everyone who hears it and heeds it and acts according to it, they[18] will leave the path of crookedness and their souls will be saved. I say to you that the Virgin will ask her beloved Son to cancel sins and write his name in the Book of Life.

Now, my beloved children, if you heed what I have advised you; the Virgin will intercede on your behalf with her beloved Son and he will crush your enemies under your feet and you will trample on the head of the monster and you will break the power of the enemy. If you heed what I have advised you, the kings and governors will offer you gifts, archons will give you honours. Berbers/Barbarians will submit to you. Use all your strength to say your prescribed prayers of the day and the night.

---

18 The Arabic does what English often does: from 'he who ... ' to 'they will', where the second pronoun is, strictly speaking, non-anaphoric.

Take care not to change the rule which I have imposed on you so that you will not be under a great judgement. Heed all that I have advised you, my beloved children, that you may be children of the kingdom of Heaven. Take care not to talk during Mass, for this is a grave error. Though singing and reading of the sermon in church are for the benefit of the souls, people engage in conversation. Everybody who talks in church, let him know that he is not acceptable to God and His angels and the Mother of God will be angry with him. His prayer will be rejected by God and he will be required to answer for his disobedience. Let nobody act in this church except those consecrated. Advise your children who come after you for future generations that nobody should speak in the sanctuary in the language of the hegira. Anyone who does this will be cursed. I have said these things to you, my beloved children. He who hears and heeds will be saved."

After he had finished his discourse, our holy father Anba Samuel, and those present heard him, Bishop Gregory wept bitterly until his garments were soaked in his tears because of what was imminent. Anba Samuel said to him, "My son, this is a minor punishment from God to the people of this generation. If the correct punishment of their sins which they have committed were visited upon them, who could resist, as it is written, "If you pay attention to sin, o Lord, who can stand before You?" [19]

In addition, as it is written, "It is good for me that you have humiliated me that I may observe your laws" and "The Lord has punished me severely, but to death has not delivered me." [20]Whoever accepts the punishment of the Lord thankfully and confesses his sins, he will not return there again. for everyone who accepts the punishment of the Lord thankfully and patiently will be saved.

---

19 Ps. 130,3
20 Ps. 119 (I cannot be more specific, and this may be the wrong place)

When it (punishment) comes to him because of the Messiah, he will be saved, as the Holy Gospel says, "He who is patient until the end will be saved." [21]But he who is not patient and doubts, woe to him forever. Many Christians in that time will deny Christ for a short time that does not last. Some deny Christ because of troubles they experience, because they do not find anyone to teach them and encourage them in their troubles. They are without the help of teaching. Many fall because the world is too much for them and their reason is bound by it. There is no-one to refute them and they fall. Some fall because of pleasure in eating and drinking only. Some fall because of idleness and sin. Then their brothers and wives do not weep for them or grieve over them, but glory in them and eat and drink with them. Thereafter they will envy them and become like them. Like them they will deny Christ. Woe to those who are like them, for their place in hell is a deep well forever."

Gregory said to him, "My holy father, do you think the matter will take some time? How long will this difficulty last and how long will this nation be dominant in Egypt?" Samuel replied, "My father Gregory, nobody knows how times are regulated and change, except the Creator alone. But if the Christians are good and turn aside from their wicked works and fulfill the laws of the Church, but follow them carefully, attentively and uprightly before God, God will lift these tribulations from them. But if they are not good, then the kingdom of the hegira will continue for generations until a king called Lasmarini, the numerical value of his name being 666. [22]Let the one who has a heart understand. He is born of two nations. The earth will be

---

21 Luke 21,19

22 F.Nau, in a note following Ziadeh's publication on p 407, offers an explanation of how the number 666 can be determined, but I am unable to understand it. For the identification with Mametios, whose name does add up to 666, see R. Griveau in *ROC* 19 p. 442. It occurs to me that if one in fact reads Lasmarini, it is possible that this name is a hybrid Arabic-Coptic name meaning 'the one dark of (al-asmar) aspect (eine)

disturbed in the days of his reign. His garments will be gold-coloured. He will be audacious in his soul and will take a man's life for a dinar.[23] There will be no peace in his time. His face will be lifeless. He is unaware of the fear of God. He has no memory. He does not carry out the laws of his father, because he is an Isma'ili and his mother has no religion, for she is a foreigner (Frankish). He is a friend of drunkenness and is bloodthirsty. People will suffer much in his days. He will kill many people unexpectedly. There will be great strain in these days, awaiting the mercy of God from many trials inflicted on them by the sons of Isma'il. [24]Afterwards, the Lord will think of his people which has suffered so much humiliation and He will send against them the Byzantine [25]King in great anger from the direction of the sea, for Michael the Archangel will appear to him in a vision and will say to him, "Arise and reject captivity, for God has made you King over the whole land. Thus, he will possess the whole land. The King of the Abyssinians will cause great destruction in the land of their fathers in the direction of the east. The hegira will flee to the deserts where they were before. They will flee before the King of the Abyssinians from the east. The Byzantine King will descend upon the son of Isma'il and surround them in the Wady el Hafar,[26] home of their fathers. He will destroy them from the western side and disperse them. Great fear and alarm will fall upon the sons of Isma'il and everyone who seeks shelter with them. God will deliver them to the Byzantine King and he will destroy them with the blade of the sword. He will take

---

23 One can merely speculate that this is an echo of Rev. 6,6, where the χοινιξ σιτου δηναριου usually understood to be the living ration for a day.

24 A reference to the Fatimids? I wonder if the burning of Baylon actually refers to the burning of Fustat, ordered by the vizier Shawar to prevent it from falling into the hands of the Crusader Amalric (a story allegedly recorded by al Maqrizi).

25 The Arabic term is 'rûm', a fairly standard way of referring to the Eastern Roman Empire. The standard Semitic way of referring to Greeks was 'yunân', also the term used in Coptic oueeienin

26 Could this be the place now known as Hafar al Batin in the NE of the country, formerly a stop-off place on the pilgrimage route to Mecca.

them prisoner because they have destroyed the land. For this reason, in the interests of justice, God will deliver them to the Byzantine King, and he will be hard on them, a hundred times more in truth than they themselves were. They will be subject to poverty, hardship, distress, rising prices and the sword. The Byzantine King will enter the land of Egypt and burn the city of the Egyptians called Babylon because the sons of Isma'il are in it. They have performed defiled acts and ruined the land of Al Jouf[27]. He will chastise the sons of Isma'il with slavery and many tribulations. Those of them who remain will flee to the desterts of their fathers. The King of Abyssinia will marry the daughter of the Byzantine King and there will be peace, quiet and harmony in the land for forty years such as one has not seen on earth. There will be great rejoicing among Christians, who will open the doors of their churches in public, they will build houses, plant vineyards, build tall buildings and rejoice in the Lord God. Woe to those who call upon the hegira in these days.

After the forty years these are the signs of the wicked king. (The first sign): the springs and rivers will turn to blood and will remain so for an hour; their water will be bitter. The second sign: babies will speak when they are three months old. The third sign: during the harvest blood will spring from the ground. The wise will flees to the hills. After that, the nation will come forth which is isolated in the part of the earth from the Arabs, they are the repellent Hagog and Magog.[28]

The earth will tremble before them and men will flee to the hills, the caves, the graveyards. They will die of hunger and thirst. This nation will defile the earth for five months. After that God will send His angel to exterminate them in an hour. The Byzantine King will take possession of the land for one year and

---

27 Does this simply mean 'empty space' or is the province in S. Arabia on the border with Jordan?

28 Eschatological figures/places known in Judaism, Christianity and Islam and even found their way into the traditions of Britain and Ireland.

six months. He will live in Jerusalem. After that God will remove the King from the face of the earth. Then the Evil One will appear, the False Messiah. He will make many signs with vain display[29]. If he can, he will lead astray the best of friends, as it is written.[30] Ten Byzantine Kings[31] will support him and will be a single counsel for him. They will strengthen him. Blessed is the one who opposes him and overcomes him. He will be king with the Messiah in future generations forever."

I heard all these things from the lips of the holy Anba Samuel, I his disciple Apollo, and I have told them to you, my brothers. As for what he said in secret to Anba Gregorius, Anba Samuel advised me not to write it. This discourse and what I have said here is not for the brothers who know them because they have heard them from the lips of, but for future generations, on the recommendation of our father Anba Samuel. He does them and practices the will be saved. But the one who disobeys will have the reward he deserves and he will be treated and punished accordingly.

Now, my brothers, let us do what is appropriate for repentance so that we may find mercy and an open face on the day of judgement, on which God will treat everyone according to the intention of his works, whether good or bad. Merciful God will make us fit to find grace and forgivingness of our sins, through the prayers of Anba Samuel and the intercession of the Mother of God, the Eternal Virgin. Glory be to the Father, the Son and the Holy Spirit, now and at all times in the future. Amen.

The blessed sermon has been completed in the peace of the Lord. Amen.

---

29   It looks as if the copyist has misunderstood this word. After the preposition the next letter should be 'fa', which would then yield 'fantasa', corresponding to the Greek 'phantasia' and also used in VitaSam (e.g. §7 to describe the entry of Cyrus into the Fayum) to indicate 'vain display', which is clearly an extension of its meaning 'illusion, delusion, vision' (GWH Lampe *Patristic Greek Lexicon* p.1471)

30   Mat. 24,11

31   Also mentioned in the Pisentius letter published by Griveau in *ROC* 19: 321

Index of Biblical References

BIBLIOGRAPHY

Abbott, N. *The monasteries of the Fayyum* Chicago, 1937.

Abu Salih *Churches and monasteries of Egypt* (tr. B.Evetts) Oxford, 1895.

Amelineau, E. *Geographie de I 'Egypte a l'epoque copte* Paris, 1894.

Amelineau E. *Monuments pour servir a l'histoire de l'Egypte chretienne* Paris, 1895 (Memoires de la Mission Archeologique Frangaise v.4 ii)

Azadian, A., Hug,G. and Munier,H. "Notes sur le Ouady Mouellah" *Bulletin de la Societe Eoyale de Geographie d'Egypte* 18(1932): 47-63.

Baladhuri *Kitab Futuh al-Buldan* (tr.P.Hitti) New York, 1916.

Ball, J. *Egypt in the classical geographers* Cairo, 1942.

Barns, J. "A Coptic apocryphal fragment" *Journal of Theological Studies* 11(1960):70-76.

Bierbrier, M. *Tomb builders of the Pharaohs* London, 1982.

Budge, E.A.W. *Coptic martyrdoms* London, 1914.

Butler, A.J. *Ancient Coptic churches* 2v. Oxford, 1884.

Butler, A.J. *The Arab conquest of Egypt* Oxford, 1902.

Callender, J. "Coptic locative constructions" *Journal of Egyptian Archaeology* 59(1973): 190-198.

Cauwenbergh, P. van *Etude sur les moines d 'Egypte* Paris, 1914.

Charles, R. *Apocrypha and pseudepigrapha of the O.T.* 2v. Oxford, 1965.

Crum, W. *A Coptic dictionary* Oxford, 1939.

Crum, W. *Coptic mss. from the Fayyum* London, 1893.

Crum, W. and Steindorff, G. *Koptische Rechtsurkunden des 8. Jahrhunderts aus Djeme* Leipzig, 1912.

Crum. W. "A Nubian prince in an Egyptian monastery" *Studies presented to F.Ll.Griffith* London, 1932.

Daressy, G. "Takinash" *Annales du Service* 18(1919): 26-28.

Drescher, J. Graeco-Coptica" *Le Museon* 82(1969):85-100

83(1970):139-155

89(1976):307-321.

Evelyn-White, H. *History of the monasteries of Nitria and Scetis* New York, 1932.

Evelyn-White, H. *Monasteries of the Wadi 'n Natrun: architecture and archaeology* New York, 1932.

Evetts, B. "Rite copte de la prise d'habit et de la profession monacale" *Revue de l'Orient Chrétien* 11(1960):60-93.

Fakhry, A. "The monastery of Kalamun" *Annates du Service* 46 (1947):63-68.

Fakhry, A. *Oases of Egypt: the Siwa oasis* Cairo, 1973.

Frend, W. *Rise of the monophysite movement* Cambridge, 1972.

Griffith, F.Ll. *Hieratic papyri from Kahun and Gurob* London, 1898.

Horner, G. *Service for the consecration of church and altar* London, 1902.

Hyvernat, H. *Actes des martyres de l'Egypte* Paris, 1886.

Hyvernat, H, *Checklist of Coptic mss. in the Pierpont Morgan Library* New York, 1919.

Johnson, A. and West, L. *Byzantine Egypt: economic studies* Princeton, 1949.

Jones, D. *The economy and administration of Egyptian monasteries* Oxford (D.Phil.thesis), 1982.

Junge, F. "Zur Funktion des sdm.hr.f" *Journal of Egyptian Archaeology* 58(1972):133-139.

Kahle, P. *Deir el Bala'izah* Oxford, 1954.

Kasser, R. *Complements au dictionnaire copte* Cairo, 1964.

Kasser, R. "Complements morphologiques au dictionnaire copte" *Bulletin de l'Institut Franqais d'Archeologie Orientate* 64 (1966):19-66.

Kosack, W. *Legende im Koptischen* Bonn, 1970.

Kuhn, K. *Panegyric on John the Baptist* Louvain, 1966.

Kuhn. K. "Some observations in the Coptic Gospel according to Thomas" *Le Museon* 73(1960):317-323.

Lampe, G. *Patristic Greek lexicon* Oxford, 1961.

Lantschoot, A. *Receuil des colophons des mss. chretiens de l'Egypte* Paris, 1929.

Lee, G. "'Perhaps' in Greek and Coptic" *Le Museon* 83(1970):137.

Liddell, H. and Scott, R. (rev. H.S.Jones) *A Greek-English lexicon* Oxford, 1961.

Maspero, J. *Histoire des patriarches d'Alexandrie* Paris, 1923

Meinardus, O. *Christian Egypt: faith and life* Cairo, 1970.

Meinardus, O. *Monks and monasteries* Cairo, 1961.

Migne, J.P. *Patrologia graeca* Paris, 1857-1912.

Müller, C. "Benjamin I, 38. Patriarch von Alexandrien" *Le Muséon* 69 (1956):313-340.

Müller, C. *Die Homilie Uber die Hochzeit zu Kana* Heidelberg, 1968.

Müller, C. "Neues Uber Benjamin I, 38. und Agathon, 39. Patriarchen von Alexandrien" *Le Museon* 72(1959):323-347.

Orlandi, T. *Quattro omelie* Milan, 1977.

Pereira, F. *Vida do Abba Samuel* Lisbon, 1894.

Petersen, Th. "The paragraph mark in Coptic illuminated ornament" *Studies presented to Bella da Costa Greene* (ed. D. Miner) Princeton, 1956.

Quecke, H. *Untersuchungen zum koptischen Stundengebet* Louvain, 1970.

Reymond, E. and Barns, J. *Four martyrdoms from the Pierpont Morgan Coptic codices* Oxford, 1973.

Schenke, H-M. "On the Middle Egyptian dialect" *Enchoria* 8 (1978) Sbd: 89-104.

Sethe, K. *Aegyptische Lesestucke* Leipzig, 1924.

Simon, J. "Fragments d'un homelie copte en 11honneur de Samuel de Kalamon" *Miscellanea Biblica* II(1934):161-178.

Simon, J. "Le monastere de Samuel de Kalamon" *Orientalia Christiana Periodica* 1(1935):46-52.

Simon, J. "St Samuel de Kalamon et son monastere dans la litterature ethiopienne" *Aethiopica* 1(1935):36-40.

Till, W. *Koptische Dialektgrammatik* Munich, 1961.

Till, W. *Koptische Grammatik* Leipzig, 1955.

Walters, C. *Monastic archaeology in Egypt* Warminster, 1974.

Wilson, M. *Coptic future tenses* The Hague, 1970. *Worterbuch der gyptischen Sprache* (ed. Erman and Grapow) Leipzig, 1926-1931.

Ziadeh, J. "Apocalypse de Samuel" *Rev.Or.Ch.* 20(1915):374-403.

A. Alcock
THE LIFE OF SAMUEL OF KALAMUN

This previously unpublished Coptic text is a hagiographical account of the life of a Coptic monk who lived between about 597 and 695 AD. He entered the monastery of Scetis at the age of 18 but when the Emperor Heraclius sent an agent to impose a new Christological doctrine upon the Copts in 631 AD, he was driven by persecution and torture first to the Fayyum and then, several years later, into the desert, where he spent three years as a captive of the Berbers, in the Siwa Oasis. On his release he founded a monastery at Kalamun where he remained as Abbot for 57 years. Although there is no direct mention of the Arab invasion of Egypt in the text, an incident is related which might be an indirect reference to it. This Coptic text with translation and notes will be useful to any student of the language or history of mediaeval Egypt.